$6 \times {}^{10}/_9 - {}^{8}/_{12}$

Native American Biographies

GERONIMO

APACHE FREEDOM FIGHTER

Spring Hermann

James Edgar
and
Jean Jessop Hervey
Point Loma Branch Library

Enslow Publishers, Inc.

40 Industrial Road
Box 398
Berkeley Heights, NJ 07922
USA

PO Box 38
Aldershot
Hants GU12 6BP
UK

http://www.enslow.com

For Bette Jane, Jean, Tillie, Pat, David, and Sandy—
like Geronimo, never taken in battle.

Library of Congress Cataloging-in-Publication Data

Hermann, Spring.
 Geronimo: Apache freedom fighter / Spring Hermann.
  p. cm.—(Native American biographies)
 Includes bibliographical references and index.
 Summary: Examines the life of the Apache chief Geronimo, who led
one of the last Indian uprisings.
 ISBN 0-89490-864-2
 1. Geronimo, 1829–1909—Juvenile literature. 2. Apache Indians—
Biography—Juvenile literature. 3. Apache Indians—Kings and rulers—
Biography. 4. Apache Indians—Wars—Juvenile literature. [1. Geronimo,
1829–1909. 2. Apache Indians—Biography. 3. Indians of North
America—Biography.] I. Title. II. Series.
E99.A6G32434   1997
979'.004972—dc20   96-25703
                                                        CIP
                                                        AC

Printed in the United States of America

10 9 8 7 6 5 4

Photo Credits: Courtesy of the Arizona Historical Society/Tucson, pp.
12, 46, 50, 61; Courtesy of the National Archives, pp. 14, 21, 27, 36, 59,
65, 71, 85, 93, 101; Spring Hermann, pp. 88, 95.

Cover Photo: Courtesy of the National Archives

CONTENTS

GERONIMO IS NAMED IN BATTLE

In the summer of 1850 in Apacheria—the land now called southern Arizona, New Mexico, and northern Mexico, then occupied by Apache— the hot, dry climate did not prevent its residents from traveling. As children, Apaches learned to make long journeys on foot, carrying a minimal amount of food and water. In this rugged, hilly land the Apaches hunted deer, rabbit, antelope, and other game; pounded the mesquite bean into meal; roasted the mescal cactus; and ate the saguaro cactus fruit.

❖Young Warrior❖

That summer the band of Apaches called the Bedonkohes (Bee-DON-ko-hays) prepared to travel. Among them was a young warrior named Goyahkla.[1] Apache words are hard to pronounce for non-Apaches, so scholars continue to disagree on how to say this name. Most say it "Goy-AHTH-lay," which means "one who yawns," or "one who is clever." At about twenty-five years old, Goyahkla already took care of his widowed mother, Juana, his wife, Alope, their daughter, Juanita, their son, Roberto, and a baby too young to be properly named.[2] He prepared his family to join the others in their band by packing the hides and furs they had tanned and cured for trade.[3] The family followed the lead of their headman, Mangas Coloradas ("Red Sleeves"), who also led the Mimbrenos from an area east of the Bedonkohes.

❖Raiding in Mexico❖

Most Apache warriors knew the routes into the Mexican states of Sonora and Chihuahua well. For centuries, the Mexicans and Apaches had raided each other's settlements and stolen each other's men, women, and children into slavery. The Spanish arrived in Apacheria at the end of the sixteenth century and started the practice. At that time, the Spanish tried to enslave the natives they found, and make them laborers in the silver and copper mines.[4] The Apaches were proud to be free and refused to accept slavery. They sought revenge. For two hundred years, Apache boys had become respected warriors by joining raiding parties and taking Mexican cattle and horses. Goyahkla had impressed Alope's father by presenting him with the many horses he had taken during a Mexican raid. These horses became Goyahkla's marriage gift, which, by Apache custom, had to be presented to a girl's father to allow her to marry.

❖Peace in Effect❖

Since the Apaches had become superior fighters to the Mexicans, the states of Sonora and Chihuahua (in Mexico) had hired a paid militia (armed fighters) to reduce these raids. Sonora passed a "scalp bounty law" in 1835, offering to pay one hundred pesos for an Apache scalp—proof of murder.[5] Chihuahua passed a similar law in 1837, offering one hundred pesos for a male scalp, fifty for a female, and twenty-five for a child's. A peso was almost equal to an American dollar at that time. By 1850, however, a peace agreement was in effect in Chihuahua. This is why Mangas Coloradas decided it was safe for warriors to bring their families on a trading trip.

Goyahkla was powerfully built, over five feet eight inches tall, with a square jaw. His dark, intense eyes, long black hair, and straight mouth gave him a fierce appearance.

Goyahkla excelled as a warrior and planned to serve his people in battle.[6] Yet, he was an affectionate man who loved his wife, Alope, his children, his many cousins, and his widowed mother. He wanted Alope and his mother to take home the bright cloth, beads, knives, and cooking items offered by the Mexican traders.

❖To the Trading Center❖

The band's final destination was a trading center called Casas Grandes in Chihuahua, Mexico. First, they camped farther north outside a village called Janos. There, the Mexican government had promised to distribute gifts to the Apaches in honor of the peace. Mangas Coloradas chose a dense patch of trees on the Janos River and set up camp for the women and children. The next morning, leaving a few men to guard the families, horses, and weapons, Mangas, Goyahkla, and about fifty warriors walked to the village.[7]

❖Officials Meet❖

The meeting between Chihuahua government officials and Apache warriors went well. The warriors ate some food and received supplies and bags of corn meal. But the prize of the day was mescal (liquor distilled from the agave cactus), which was much stronger than the tizwin (corn whisky) that the

Apaches distilled for themselves. Men from the Chihuahua government rode out and gave mescal to the men who acted as guards at the Apache camp. Soon everyone was somewhat drunk.

❖Disaster Strikes❖

Later that afternoon, Goyahkla and the other warriors walked back toward their camp, toting gifts and still feeling the effects of the mescal. Suddenly a few Apache women and children ran out from behind bushes. They told the men the terrible news. A force of Mexican militia and scouts had surprised their camp while the guards were sleepy from the mescal. The militia killed all the guards, captured the horses and weapons, and destroyed supplies.[8] Worst of all, these soldiers shot many women and children and took their scalps. They also captured others to sell as slaves.

Goyahkla's family was either murdered or captured. He did not know which. Mangas Coloradas took charge. The soldiers could be waiting to ambush the Apaches. He ordered the warriors to hide with the surviving women and children. After dark, with others standing guard, each man crept through the camp. Goyahkla's worst fear came true: his mother, wife, and three children were among the slain.[9] Later in his life, Goyahkla recalled turning away from the bodies in silent shock and standing beside the river for a long time. Eventually the other warriors formed a council away from the camp. Goyahkla had to take his place.

The loss was terrible. At least twenty-one people had been killed (although the Apaches' full count is not known) and about sixty-two women and children had been taken captive.[10] Witnesses identified the soldiers as a Sonoran militia led by their new commander, General José María Carrasco, hungry for revenge and scalp bounty.

Chihuahua citizens would not fight their neighbor's soldiers on behalf of the Apaches. With wounded survivors, no weapons, supplies, or pack horses, Mangas Coloradas and the council decided that they would head for home immediately. This meant that Goyahkla could not give his family a proper burial. They would not easily descend to Usen (the Apache god) in the next life.

Goyahkla waited as all passed him by. Mangas Coloradas was headman, and his orders were for the good of the survivors. Goyahkla turned from the site where his family lay in a pool of their own blood. He recalled: "I did not pray nor did I resolve to do anything . . . for I had no purpose left. I finally followed the tribe in silence."[11]

◈ Going Home ◈

After three nights of forced marches, the Bedonkohes made it to the Mexican border. As they rested, Goyahkla spoke to other warriors who had left behind dead loved ones. He discovered that he was the only one who had lost every member of his family.

When Goyahkla and the surviving Bedonkohes arrived at their home settlement on the upper Gila River, they performed the Apache ritual of burying or destroying the deceased people's belongings.[12] This custom came from the Apache belief that "sickness could be contracted . . . from touching the deceased's possessions."[13] Goyahkla burned his family's antelope-hide tipi with the lovely painted decorations Alope had made. Then he held the playthings of his three children. These toys should have been buried with them, to comfort them on their journey to Usen. But the Mexicans had taken that chance away. So Goyahkla burned them also, feeling his heart "ache for revenge upon Mexico."[14]

❖On the Warpath❖

The survivors of the Janos raid would take the warpath against the Mexican militia that attacked them. Because Goyahkla was an able warrior, and because he had lost the most family members, he was allowed to be spokesperson. He would visit the other bands of Apaches who might be willing to send warriors on the warpath with them.

Goyahkla's first visit was to the settlement of the Chiricahua band. Relationships between bands were good. Perhaps they would join the battle. Dostehseh,

— ❖ —

After the Janos raid, Goyahkla (Geronimo) was chosen by his people as their spokesperson to approach other bands about seeking revenge on the Mexicans. Geronimo remained an inspirational leader of his people throughout his life.

a daughter of Mangas Coloradas, was a wife to their headman, Cochise. Apache custom at this time permitted a warrior to take more than one wife if he could support them. Scholars believe that Dostehseh was Cochise's first, or principal, wife.

Cochise called a council. The warriors sat in rows according to their rank. They smoked tobacco rolled in oak leaves. Goyahkla rose and told about the attack on their men, women, and children. Then he asked the Chiricahuas to join the Apaches in war, saying: "I will lead you to their city. I will fight in front of the battle. I only ask you to follow me to avenge this wrong done by these Mexicans." He concluded his speech by reminding the Chiricahuas of danger on the warpath, saying, "Men may return or be killed. I want no blame from their kinsmen, for they themselves have chosen to go. If I am killed no one need mourn for me."[15] Cochise and his council agreed to join Goyahkla's people in war.

Goyahkla then traveled to the council of the Nednais. Their headman, Juh, was a boyhood friend. Goyahkla's wife, Alope, had come from this band. These Apaches would also take the warpath. Finally, other members of the Mimbrenos (called Chichenne or "Red Paint People," for the band of red they painted on their faces for war), and the Warm Springs band under Victorio and Baishan, called Cuchillo Negro ("Black Knife") in Spanish, completed the war party.

— ⬦ —

These two young Apache warriors are ready for battle. They wear only their breechcloths, headbands, and moccasins, and carry bows and arrows. This photo was probably taken around 1880.

At this time, it is said by Apaches, that Goyahkla had his first major spiritual experience. Although he had been taught to remove arrowheads and bullets and treat wounds with healing herbs, Goyahkla was not a true medicine man or spiritual leader.[16] Yet the spirits spoke to him: "Goyahkla!" the voice called four times. "No gun can kill you. I will take the bullets from the guns of the Mexicans, so they will have nothing but powder. And I will guide your arrows."[17]

Now Goyahkla was empowered by spirits and by vengeance. He became what we might call psychic. From then on, he seemed to know where the enemy hid and when his people were in danger. This new power was well noted by Apaches.

❖War Party Sets Out❖

Late during the fall of 1850, the large Apache war party went south. Running as much as forty miles a day, they traveled undetected through the mountains. They slipped down the canyons of Sonora to the town of Arispe. Each warrior wore a breechcloth, a simple cloth that passed between the legs and fell in back and front from a belt around the waist. High moccasins protected their legs and feet. They also wore belts to hold arrows, spears, and knives. They carried a pouch with a bit of dried food. Twisted cloth headbands held back their long hair. They took no horses, to avoid leaving tracks. At Arispe they found the two units of cavalry and the two units of infantry that had massacred their families.

Goyahkla sent forth a decoy party. Eight Mexicans rode out from Arispe to see if this decoy was a raiding party. The Apaches quickly knifed and scalped the eight Mexicans, in an attempt to draw the entire militia into battle.

❖Geronimo Takes His Name❖

Those Apache warriors still hidden outside of town attacked and captured a wagon-and-mule supply train filled with rifles and ammunition. This helped to balance the odds, since the Mexican militia had most of the firepower. The Apache warriors waited the night. They prayed for guidance in battle, as they always did when facing an enemy. Conducting war was a holy ritual.

The next day, all of the Mexican militia units marched out onto a field in a show of power. The Apaches preferred hiding, entrapping, and then fighting. Now they would need new tactics, since they were outnumbered and outarmed. Goyahkla went to the headmen and asked to be war chief. He had the skill, the power, and the anger. He prayed to prove himself worthy of their trust.[18]

Goyahkla split up his men and spread them out into a half-moon shape along the river. There they found cover under some trees. As the infantry and cavalry rushed into the center of the crescent,

Apache warriors spread farther out. Suddenly they encircled the militia and attacked from the rear. At the head of all the charges stood Goyahkla, screaming the battle instructions. He fought with a knife in one hand and a spear in the other. The warriors fought until their guns were emptied, their arrows spent, and their spears broken in the bodies of their enemy. As the spirit voice promised, bullets flew all around Goyahkla. Some nicked him, but none killed him.

At each charge, the Mexican militia lost many men. The soldiers recognized Goyahkla from earlier raids. They feared his fierce war whoop. They began to call out: "Geronimo!" Perhaps they were asking for help from their patron saint, Jerome. At each charge, the men cried "Geronimo!" over and over, until Goyahkla took it as his battle name.

At last it was over. Geronimo told of it later:

> *Still covered with the blood of my enemies, still holding my conquering weapon, still hot with the joy of battle, victory, and vengeance, I was surrounded by the Apache braves and made war chief. Then I gave the orders for scalping the slain.*[19]

The Apaches spoke of nothing but the greatness in battle of the man now called Geronimo. They felt avenged. But the man called Geronimo would never give up his ongoing war. He would never forgive his Mexican enemy. Other Apache leaders, worn and starved after decades of war, would make peace treaties with enemies yet to come. Geronimo would endure past them all.[20]

Although he married other wives and fathered other children, Geronimo never forgot his first family. He grieved forever over the loss of his wife and for the childhood that his first three children never enjoyed—an Apache childhood like his own.

GERONIMO GROWS UP

A celebration swept through the Bedonkohe band each time a child was born. This small group of people, who often lost members to disease or wounds received on raids, treasured each child. A boy was born to Taklishim, a respected warrior, and his wife, Juana. According to Apache tradition, and to the research done by the director of the Museum of Fort Sill, Oklahoma, this boy was the grandson of the great Nednai Apache headman Mahko and his first wife.[1] Mahko's band, the Nednais, lived in the Sierra Madre mountains. For the most part, Mahko kept peace with the Spanish who shared this area with him. He raised horses and corn and helped his fellow tribesmen.[2] When Mahko's son Taklishim married, this young man joined Juana's Bedonkohes. Apache custom said the husband should join his wife's people.

❖Life as a Child❖

Geronimo, then called Goyahkla, was born where the Middle Fork of the Gila River joins the West Fork, near the Gila cliff dwellings in today's southwestern New Mexico. However, no clear maps of this area existed in the 1820s. Apaches did not need one to find their way over the vast expanse of Apacheria.[3] Taklishim had two sisters, whose daughters, Nahthletla and Ishton, grew up as close as siblings to Goyahkla. It is said that this little boy had half brothers called Porico and Fun, and a sister called Nahdoste. But these could also be first cousins instead.

Goyahkla lived in his parents' tipi, a wood frame covered with animal hides to form a sturdy tent.[4] When Apaches moved to follow herds of game during warm weather, they built a more simple shelter of saplings and brush called a wickiup. Entrances to Apache homes always faced east to the rising sun.

An infant carrier called a "tosch," or a cradleboard, was built for babies like Goyahkla. It consisted of a frame, crosspieces, a canopy to shield the baby's

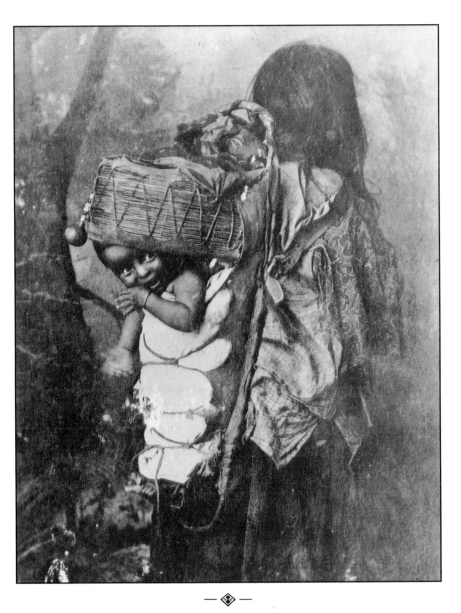

— ❖ —

This photograph titled "Apache squaw and papoose in cradleboard" was taken sometime in the last half of the nineteenth century. This method of carrying an Apache baby still had not changed since Geronimo was carried by his mother in the 1820s.

face, and a footrest. Buckskin covered the canopy and the frame. Decorations differing for boys and girls were painted on it. Bedding of wild mustard plants was used, and it was thrown away each time the baby wet it.[5] Mothers attached a strong strap called a tumpline to hang the tosch from a bough, sling it on their back, or carry it on horseback.

◈ Cradle Ceremony ◈

When the cradleboard was completed, a special "cradle ceremony" was held for family and friends. The shaman, a specially trained medicine person who performed all Apache religious rites, blessed the baby with corn pollen, then threw pollen to the four directions. After more rituals, a special person was selected to place the baby in his cradle. A feast and social gathering followed.[6]

After Goyahkla learned to walk, his family probably gave him the "Putting on Moccasins" ceremony, where the baby was blessed with songs, prayers, and special pollen when he received his first shoes.[7] Moccasins became an Apache's most important item of clothing. More like a soft-soled boot, the moccasins' thick hide protected the wearer from rocks and thorns. They could be pulled up high for warmth. Men carried a tool for making a hole, sinew thread, and leather for a sole with them in case they had to repair their moccasins. One could not get around without them.[8]

◈Hair Cutting Ceremony◈

The following spring, when Goyahkla was about two, he probably had the "Hair Cutting" ceremony. This ceremony used prayers and pollen to bless the child's first haircut. After childhood, Apache boys and girls did not cut their hair again. They wore it tied back with a headband.

◈Peaceful Times◈

Bedonkohe Apaches were not at war with white American settlers during the 1820s. The white settlers had not yet found reason to want Apache land. Some raids back and forth with Mexicans continued, but this was generally a peaceful time. Bedonkohe children were taught to help in the gardens, where they grew melons, pumpkins, beans, and maize (southwestern corn). Goyahkla recalled that his family's garden was about two acres, tilled with wooden hoes, and the unfenced fields were shared by many families.[9] Corn was ground for cornbread, nuts and berries were gathered and dried, and small game was hunted. Herbs to cure sickness and wounds had to be found. All these activities kept women and youngsters busy.

As Goyahkla grew strong, he too learned to help his family by gardening, gathering, and hunting. Little Apache boys also enjoyed playing. But, their play often involved war games or pretend hunting. Children used sunflower stalks as pretend spears and charged make-believe enemies. They hid for hours in the brush and stalked rabbits, rodents, and game birds. In this way they learned patience, cunning, and the animals' habits. Boys wrestled and built physical strength at an early age. All children became expert riders as soon as they could grab a pony's mane and climb on its back.

❖Training Begins❖

At about age ten, Goyahkla began his training program. Training would last until he was ready to join adult hunting and raiding parties. An Apache father like Tashlikim might tell his son:

> *You run to that mountain and come back. That will make you strong . . . my son, no one is your friend . . . your legs are your friends, your brain is your friend, your eyesight is your friend.*[10]

During those mountain runs, boys had to breathe through only their nostrils. To prove it, they ran both ways holding a mouthful of water.[11] Boys were told to take icy swims, or roll in snow. Daily, they jogged over rough country with a load on their backs. To build endurance, boys were made to keep watch without sleep for up to two days and nights. Their final test was a two-week wilderness experience where each boy lived alone and survived by his own skill.[12]

❖On the Hunt❖

At last, Goyahkla's father and his trainers allowed him to join adult hunting trips. He helped track herds of deer, antelope, and elk. Usually the hunters crept on foot, against the wind to hide their scent. Disguised by brush and perhaps a deerskin, Goyahkla spent hours closing in on his prey.

Goyahkla also mastered hunting wild turkey by chasing the big bird down on his pony. Just as the turkey took flight, he swung his hunting club overhead and killed the bird. Bear was also plentiful during Goyahkla's youth. If a bear attacked him, he killed it with a large knife and spear. Bearskins could make good robes. But bear meat was not to be eaten. Because the bear could walk upright like a man, it might possess spirit power.[13]

Men taught their duty to boys like Goyahkla. One's first duty was obedience and truthfulness to one's people. It was said "an Apache obeys or dies."[14] Few Apache children were ever beaten, unless they told a lie. This was because a lie could endanger others. It was an honor for a boy in training to serve another warrior. The boy would listen, watch, help, and learn. A boy had to earn the respect of the warriors. Eventually a boy realized that anyone outside the tribe was a potential enemy.

By 1840, Goyahkla was ready to prove himself as a man. He had mastered the hunter's skills. He had even ridden to the Northeast on a buffalo hunt. The hunt supplied meat and fur robes to warm the band through the cool mountain winter. His next step was to join the raiding parties that were moving against the Mexicans. At that time, the United States was arguing with Mexico over borders. So the Mexican government had few soldiers to spare to fight Apache raiders.

After two hundred years of raids upon each other, the Mexicans and Apaches were still sworn enemies. A civil war in Mexico took many lives, made worse by losses from Apache raids. Mexican officials estimated that between 1820 and 1835, at least five thousand Mexican citizens were killed. One hundred Mexican settlements were abandoned along the northern frontier.[15]

Goyahkla had been taught that the goal of a Mexican raid was to bring home horses and goods, without any injury to the raider. The European style of marching forth into open battle, as the Mexican militias did, was not for him. A smart fighter never fought in open battle when he could cleverly ambush a foe. A raider learned to be patient, use disguises, and outwit his enemy by secretly observing him for days.[16] A raider who could get away with goods without being attacked was more respected than one who stole more but lost comrades in the battle. It would take years, however, before Goyahkla became a master fighter. The stories say he tended to be too passionate

— ◈ —

This photo of Geronimo (left) and Naiche (right) with their horses was taken on the range at Fort Sill, Oklahoma. Earlier in life, Goyahkla (Geronimo) went on Mexican raids in order to bring home horses and goods for his people.

and bold. He did not always act on these teachings of patience.

⬥Becoming a Warrior⬥

Goyahkla went on the required four expeditions before he could become a warrior. Apparently he did a good job, for he was asked to join the warriors' council while still in his teens. During earlier years, Goyahkla and his family enjoyed visits back and forth with other relatives. They saw his father's former band, the Nednais, who became "devoted entirely to warfare and raiding the settlements."[17] A boy called Juh (pronounced "Whoa," which Apaches agree meant "Long Neck"), a cousin, became friendly with Goyahkla. Along with regular games and contests, Juh liked to play jokes on the girls. He and his cousin hid in the forest, watched the girls work hard to gather baskets of acorns, then snatched them away![18]

When the boys were in their teens, Juh visited Goyahkla's band. This time Juh fell in love with one of those girls he had tormented, Ishton, Goyahkla's sister (or first cousin).[19] Goyahkla was also falling in love with a girl named Alope, daughter of Naposo. The young men probably helped and encouraged each other in attracting these girls. Apache girls were very proud of their independence and modesty. These girls had their puberty ceremonies at about age four-teen. This involved an elaborate dance to celebrate their readiness to marry. After this, they stayed close to their father's tipi and waited for the man who could support them and care for them. Juh and Goyahkla had to prove themselves to these girls.

❖In Mourning❖

Goyahkla was ready to ask his father to approach Alope's parents about a marriage proposal. His father, Taklishim, however, became very ill with a fever and died. After he died, Juana, Goyahkla, and the other children went into mourning. It was the custom for friends who had watched the deceased leave this life to close his eyes, dress him in his best clothes, put special paint on his face, and wrap him in his best blanket. Then the friends laid the deceased on his best horse and led the animal into the mountains. There caves were used for burial sites. The warrior was laid to rest with his best weapons. His grave was hidden by piled stones.[20] Goyahkla offered to care for his mother and help with the other children. Apache custom allowed widows to remarry whenever they wished. Juana, however, decided to live with her son, Goyahkla, and not marry again.

❖Times Change❖

Times were changing for the Apaches. American bounty hunters were starting to track them down. These men tracked and killed Apaches to turn in their scalps. In 1837, James Johnson, one of the first

Americans to make scalping his business, had lured over two-hundred Apaches and their headman Juan José to a "feast" in what is now Hidalgo County, New Mexico. Johnson blasted the Apaches to death with hidden cannons. He personally shot Juan José. When Juan José's ally, Mangas Coloradas, and his band heard of this ambush, they became suspicious of any white American, whom they called "white-eyes."

By 1846, the United States went to war against Mexico. Many white soldiers started traveling through what is now Texas and New Mexico. Some Apaches decided to trust these white-eyes, because they had a common enemy. If both were trying to raid and kill Mexicans, they must have a bond between them.

Rebel Apache Don Santiago Kirker made a secret pact with Governor Angel Trias of Chihuahua, Mexico. Kirker turned on his own Apache people, and with a small army of renegades, murdered hundreds of Apache, mostly in the Sierra Madres where the Nednais lived.[21]

❖Raiding Traditions❖

When the white soldiers conquered all of the territory they called "New Mexico," they ordered the Native Americans (Apaches, Comanches, and Navajos) to stop raiding Mexican ranches and towns. But raiding not only satisfied the centuries-old need for revenge, it also fed these people. Mules and horses that they stole provided meat. During these times, the buffalo and large game were disappearing or moving north into the territories of other tribes. So the Apaches learned to eat horse and mule meat in place of game. Raiding had become honorable and necessary for all of the Native Americans of the Southwest.

Goyahkla had another reason to keep raiding. He had gone to Alope's parents with a marriage proposal. According to Apache custom, a boy's father or relative went to the girl's father and asked how many marriage gifts the father wanted. Goyahkla, without a father or male relative, decided to march up to Naposo and speak for himself. Naposo supposedly asked for many horses.

The only way Goyahkla could marry Alope was to go on a raid and bring back horses. This was not an easy thing for a young warrior to do on his own. Although few words had passed between them, Goyahkla believed Alope loved him also. But how would he satisfy her demanding father without getting himself killed?

Geronimo Sees the White Man Arrive

Goyahkla found the nerve to speak for himself to Alope's father. He would not, however, have been so improper as to speak to Alope. Later in his life, Goyahkla told the story about raiding a Mexican ranch near Tres Alamos. Two of the youngest warriors in his band, eager to show their own skill, agreed to join him. He did not say that this raid was to gain his marriage gifts, but it may have been. The three young men were able to steal horses and cattle by shooting flaming arrows into the roof of the house and "smoking out" the ranch hands who were inside.

Inexperienced Goyahkla had *not* been careful enough, however, to avoid the ranch hands who had run for help and waited for him. The raid had been bold, but Goyahkla's retreat was unplanned. He and his friends were later ambushed while trying to drive the stock back up to their home territory. Goyahkla's friends were killed.[1]

The next raid Goyahkla led was probably to redeem his pride. Later, he recalled the other warriors turning their backs on him for losing his companions. But he managed to come up with the marriage gifts. As was the custom, he tied the horses outside the tipi of Naposo. This gift was approved by Alope's father, and the bride herself.

✦ Apache Marriages ✦

Once Apache families agreed on a marriage, they performed no special ritual or ceremony. Alope, her mother, and female relatives built the marriage tipi and decorated it with paintings on the hides.[2] As soon as the home was prepared, Goyahkla and Alope moved in together and started a family.

Now Goyahkla had to hunt and provide for his wife, and perhaps even help out with her family. But one social law existed among the Apache people. The groom was to avoid his mother-in-law forever. As a rule, most Apache men avoided their wives' fathers and grandmothers also.[3]

❖White Men Arrive❖

In October 1846, the Apaches noticed a strange group of white men riding through their country. We know that headman Mangas Coloradas, and probably Goyahkla, met these white men. They were the advance guard of the United States Army of the West. They were lead by General Stephen Kearny, along with officers W. H. Emory and A. L. Johnston. These soldiers may have been the first white men ever seen by these Apaches. This meeting took place near the Santa Rita copper mines, in Mimbreno-Bedonkohe territory.

After centuries of being captured and released by Mexicans, many Apaches, including Goyahkla, spoke basic Spanish. Through this language, the headmen communicated with a white man, who translated for all. They traded mules for goods. Two white officers recalled in their journals the reactions of the Apaches when they learned that the army was going to wage war against Mexico. Mangas Coloradas, Goyahkla's headman, told the officers:

> *You have taken Santa Fe, let us go on and take Chihuahua and Sonora. We will go with you. You fight for the soil, we fight for plunder; so we will agree perfectly.*[4]

— ◈ —

Apache territory, in the southeastern mountains of Arizona, near Fort Bowie, is shown here. United States troops moved into Apache territory in order to wage war on the Mexicans. The Apaches failed to become allies with the United States Army, in spite of having a common enemy.

It was not then the policy of the United States Army to join forces with Native Americans, although such unions had been tried a few times in the past. General Kearny and his officers were not going to ally themselves with the Apaches. They were under orders to subdue them and return their Mexican captives.

When General Kearny had taken Santa Fe, he told the residents, who were no longer Mexican citizens, that he would not expect them to help him fight against their own people. But he noted that the Mexican government had allowed the Apaches and Navajos to "carry off your sheep, and even your women, whenever they please. My government will correct all this. It will keep off the Indians, protect you in your persons and property."[5]

Kearny took the point of view that the Native Americans were to blame for all of the Mexicans' troubles. He did not note, however, that the Mexicans had carried on the same kind of raids against Apaches.

The Apache headmen gave assurance that the white soldiers could pass through their territory unharmed. They would even be offered food. One of General Kearny's scouts was a man who would later become famous for rounding up the entire Navajo tribe into captivity. His name was Christopher "Kit" Carson. At this time he advised General Kearny: "I would not trust one of them."[6]

The Apache bands continued to raid ranches throughout their old territories. But much of the land was now under the control of the United States Army. From 1846 to 1850, along with their distant relatives the Navajos, the Apaches reportedly "ran off more than 12,000 mules, 7,000 horses, 31,000 cattle, and upwards of 450,000 sheep from New Mexico."[7] During this time, the United States government won these territories from Mexico through warfare. The Treaty of Guadalupe Hidalgo, ratified in 1848, ended the war with Mexico. It turned much of the Southwest over to the United States government.[8]

❖Apaches Not Citizens❖

Also at this time, the Apaches and Navajos were legally made "wards of the government." They were not citizens but had to do what the government told them. Governor Charles Bent of New Mexico was put in charge of the Native Americans who lived in his territory. The concept of once "belonging" to the Mexican government and now "belonging" to the United States government was unheard of to the Native Americans. As far as they understood, the creator had led them to this place first and made it their homeland. The Apache people answered to no one but Usen, their creator.

Goyahkla and his fellow Bedonkohes met the Boundary Commission around 1851. The Commission was trying to determine the line that now divided New

Mexico Territory (the term for what is now all of New Mexico and Arizona) from Old Mexico (the states of Chihuahua and Sonora). Finding where the new boundary would run between the United States and Mexico would take a lot of time. Much of this territory was called "uninhabited," meaning it had no whites living in it. It had not been properly mapped by whites.

Goyahkla recalled that this time they had no good interpreter, but they made peace by shaking hands. They traded buckskins, blankets, and horses for shirts and food supplies. The Apaches also brought game they had shot. In exchange the white men gave them money. Goyahkla did not know the value of this money. He later learned from the Navajo how to use it. Each day the white men measured the land with strange instruments, and put down marks that Goyahkla could not understand.[9]

❖The Boundary Commission❖

The Boundary Commission was headed by John Russell Bartlett. He was accompanied by two other men. None of these men had any experience dealing with Native Americans. John C. Cremony, a Boston newspaper reporter who spoke Spanish, recorded his impressions of this group. They always dressed formally despite the heat, and rode inside a large carriage filled with repeating rifles.

Mangas Coloradas, Goyahkla, and the others camped about two miles from the inactive copper mines. They visited often, said Cremony, "to observe our movements and to practice their skill in begging."[10] To a white man from Boston, the Native American practice of constant bartering for goods may have looked like "begging." To an Apache like Goyahkla, it was a way of testing the strength and perseverance of these outsiders. They had been using such an approach with the Mexicans for a century.

Cremony had previously traveled into the Southwest in 1847. He had formed a certain respect for the Apache warrior. He said:

> No amount of cold, hunger or thirst seems to have any appreciable affect upon an Apache. Whatever his sufferings, not complaint or murmur is ever heard to escape his lips.[11]

Cremony noted that he was the only member of the Commission with whom the Apaches could communicate in Spanish, so his tent "became their headquarters for visits, which became almost daily for several consecutive months."[12] To keep peace, Bartlett had a suit of clothing made for the powerful headman, Mangas Coloradas. It was said that Mangas received his Spanish name ("Red Sleeves") because during his days in battle, his sleeves were red up to the elbows with the blood of his enemies. Bartlett described the suit as a blue broadcloth coat lined with scarlet. It was trimmed with gold buttons. The suit included pants with a strip of scarlet on the outer seam from the hips down, a white shirt and red silk sash.[13] At that time, Mangas Coloradas was willing to deal in a peaceful way with white men. That attitude was soon to change.

❖Family Life❖

During the 1840s, Goyahkla hunted, raided, traded, and looked after his family. He and his wife, Alope, had three children. They played together, surrounded by parents, grandparents, cousins, and young friends. As they grew older, Goyahkla told his children the stories of Apache origins. One favorite story was about a boy who fought a dragon, who was killing all the children, by firing four arrows into the dragon's heart.[14] This boy was a hero to Goyahkla, and was symbolic of every Apache who learned to fight cleverly but ferociously and lay down his life for his family and his tribe.

That summer, Mangas Coloradas planned a journey with Goyahkla and the other warriors into Old Mexico. The state of Chihuahua wanted peace. The citizens were offering gifts and trading opportunities. It would be a good journey, one in which the women and children would accompany the warriors.

By the end of that year, Goyahkla had seen his mother, wife, and three little children murdered at Janos in Chihuahua. He had led the avenging raid against the Sonoran militia, where he got his battle name. He had made his vow to wage war against Mexico for the rest of his life.

He had become Geronimo.

Geronimo in Battle

Geronimo's band, the Bedonkohes, had by the 1850s mainly united with the Mimbrenos. Each band centered its settlements in the same New Mexican mountain range. The Bedonkohes were living slightly to the east of the Mimbrenos, where the Mongollon Mountains became the Mimbrenos Mountains. This meant that Mangas Coloradas was regarded as headman over both bands. As a young but powerful raider and hunter, Geronimo gained the attention and favor of Mangas Coloradas. They would ride together for many years.

Geronimo had always expressed deep affection for his family. Now his parents, wife, and children were dead. His "sister" (or cousin), Ishton, had married his friend Juh, a headman with the Nednai band. Geronimo's sister Nahdoste married Nana of the Warm Springs Apaches. Geronimo's family had dispersed.

❖Another Marriage❖

As an important warrior still in his twenties, it was expected that Geronimo would soon marry again. Cheehashkish, a Bedonkohe woman who may have known Geronimo most of his life, became his next wife.[1] Together they started a new family. Tribal customs encouraged an important warrior to find a "second wife" to show his importance. This was a practical custom. There were usually more women than warriors. It made sense to the Apache for a man to support more than one wife. So in another year, Geronimo married Nanathathtith, also a Bedonkohe. Geronimo and Cheehashkish had a son named Chappo, and, later, a daughter named Dohnsay, who was nicknamed Lulu. Geronimo was also a devoted father to the children he had with wife Cheehashkish. They were strong and grew to adulthood.

❖Raids Continue❖

Throughout the 1850s and early 1860s, Geronimo raided in Mexico. Gone were the peaceful days of his youth when bands could settle, tucked away in the mountain ranges, grow crops, and tan hides. Now the Apache had to keep moving. The raiding life had become a necessity. Often they left their fine tipis of hides and poles behind and built wickiups with what brush they could cut down on the trail. With each raid, the danger to the Apaches grew. With each raid, Geronimo's desire for revenge on the Mexicans also grew. He led raiding parties with as few as three warriors, and as many as thirty.

❖Scarred Forever❖

Geronimo was nearly killed during hand-to-hand battle with a Mexican soldier during a raid in the Sierra de Sahuaripa Mountains. After he was knocked out, his life was saved by a fellow Apache warrior. The Apaches killed many, only to find their leader, Geronimo, unconscious from a blow by the butt of a Mexican trooper's gun. Geronimo's friend bathed his head with water. Weak from blood loss and a probable concussion, Geronimo was revived. He found the strength to march back to Arizona. He would wear the scar from that gun butt forever.[2]

Back at their camp, Geronimo's family nursed him to health. But his vow to continue war against the Mexicans drove him south of the border again the

— ◆ —

Geronimo is shown here, late in his life, wearing his special headdress, a finely embroidered vest, and a scarf. The decorated leather cap was trimmed with eagle feathers and ribbons. A headdress such as this was worn during healing ceremonies and at other events.

next summer. This time he found twelve warriors. They planned a raid on the Casas Grande area of northern Chihuahua, Mexico. As usual, the band was short on supplies. Geronimo hoped to raid the mule trains and drive one back up across the United States border to their camp.

Their attack was successful. But as the warriors drove the mule trains toward the border, they were surprised by Mexican cavalry troops. Geronimo was hit—"a glancing lick at the lower corner of the left eye"—which knocked him out. He regained consciousness, but later received another bullet wound in the side. Still he kept dodging and fighting. Enemy bullets could not kill him. He climbed a steep canyon where the enemy's horses could not follow. The Apache warriors split up in order to escape and survive. They all returned home, but without food or supplies.

Forced to rest while his eye and side healed, Geronimo watched his wives one morning as they cooked breakfast in their camp. Most of the warriors had gone to hunt or to trade with Navajos who lived in northern Arizona and New Mexico. Navajos were weavers of wool blankets, something the Apaches needed. Suddenly, three groups of Mexican troops, who had surrounded the camp at night, charged forward with guns blasting.

◈More Casualties◈

Stunned and half blind from his wound, Geronimo had only a bow and arrows at hand to fight back. The women and children raced for cover in the mountains. Many were shot as they fled. Cheehashkish and her children survived. Among the dead, we are told, were Geronimo's second wife Nanathathtith and their baby. Another family of Geronimo's was lost, casualties of his war with Mexico.[3]

This raid devastated the band. The Mexican soldiers stole weapons, blankets, and supplies. They also captured four women into slavery. Geronimo and the returning warriors had to struggle to keep their families alive throughout that winter. Without weapons to use for hunting, they were desperate for food. Loss of weapons also kept Geronimo from taking the warpath the following year. His determination to fight his Mexican enemies, however, did not lessen.

◈The Search for Gold◈

Throughout the 1850s, raiding between Mexicans and Apaches continued. At this time, white men searching for gold, silver, and other precious metals entered the traditional Apache hunting grounds. Apaches considered gold the symbol of the sun. It was sacred to Usen the creator. So they resented the white miners.[4] The United States government received complaints that some bands of Apaches attacked the intruders who came to dig up their earth. Not only did the Apaches want them off their land, they also wanted their mules. Mules had become a source of meat as the buffalo and big game were killed off.

Something had to be done about the growing violence between the Apaches and the miners. Superintendent Major John Greiner persuaded Mangas Coloradas and some other headmen to sign a treaty on July 1, 1852, in Santa Fe. This treaty prevented attacks on Americans traveling through or working on Apache lands. Geronimo, for unknown reasons, would not sign.[5]

The treaty held, for the most part. It not only protected the miners but also the travelers going to and from California. But no simple agreement would stop the warfare with Mexico that Geronimo, Cochise, and Nednai leader Juh actively waged. The Treaty of Guadalupe Hidalgo was ignored by Apaches when it came to Mexican attacks. It was also against international law for the Mexican soldiers to cross the border, wage war on American soil, and capture Native Americans as slaves. In the 1850s, this law existed on paper by treaty. It was not enforced, however.

Geronimo organized many raids during the mid-1850s (although when he dictated his autobiography fifty years later, he accidentally pushed the dates of events up by about eight years). Geronimo and Juh were estimated to be about the same age, in their thirties at this time, and powerful, physical fighters. Cochise was estimated to be about ten years older.

— ❖ —

The Apaches ignored the Treaty of Guadalupe Hidalgo and continued the Mexican attacks. Geronimo is the man on horseback to the left. The other rider is Naiche, son of Cochise. Some scholars say that the young man to the far left, carrying the baby, is Geronimo's son Chappo. This young man and the other one on foot are both painted for war.

Geronimo's daring in battle was well known. Juh's son Asa Daklugie, as a boy, recalled being put in Geronimo's band right after the death of his father, and then placed with Mangas (son of Mangas Coloradas) and his band. Once when Mangas's band was in trouble, Daklugie said to his brother about Mangas: "Now if he were only Geronimo! Regardless of the odds, my uncle would have taken action!"[6]

❖Raid Goes Wrong❖

Some raids went wrong, even for Geronimo. Once he led a major force of twenty warriors into Mexico. First, he relocated all of the warriors' families in a safe place. This way neither the Mexican troopers nor other hostile tribes could attack defenseless women and children. Then the warriors went into Sonora, south of Tombstone, Arizona, and made several raids. All went well, until they raided a mule train about forty-five miles from Arispe, and found it was loaded with bottles of mescal.

The warriors got drunk and fighting broke out. Geronimo was careful not to get drunk. He tried to keep command. But his orders were disobeyed. Finally, when most of the warriors lay in a stupor, Geronimo poured out the rest of the mescal. Then he found that two of the warriors were actually wounded—one by an arrow and one by a spear. He never found out how it happened. But Geronimo, skilled in treating wounds, saved both of them.

When all had sobered up, Geronimo led his people home again. For the first time, these Apaches took along some cattle they had encountered. For some reason, they had never eaten beef before. They roasted this meat and decided it was good. From then on, they added cattle to their raiding plans.[7]

Raiding made Geronimo a main figure among his people. As he rose to power, he also extended his family. Sometime during these years, Geronimo married Shegha, a Chiricahua-Nednai woman and a close relative of his friend Cochise.[8]

❖Negotiating Treaties❖

Around 1857, Dr. Michael Steck, a new Superintendent, arrived and negotiated with the Apache bands. After talking to the Mimbrenos, Warm Springs, and Mescalero bands, Steck gave presents and promised to draw up "guaranteed homelands for the Apache tribes."[9] The concept of "homelands" may not have been too clear, so these Apaches agreed. At this time we believe that Geronimo was staying with Cochise and the Chiricahuas, his wife Shegha's people. In 1858, the Chiricahuas met with Steck, who asked for protection for travelers going along the Gila Trail through Arizona to California. Steck was especially concerned about Apache Pass, a steep and dangerous crossing of the Chiricahua Mountains. The stagecoaches carrying the mail also traveled this pass. Cochise agreed to let the Overland Mail stagecoach and small parties of white men travel the Gila Trail.[10] Geronimo abided by Cochise's decision.

Steck negotiated similar deals with the Coyoteros and the Pinalenos, bands who lived in western Arizona and had already begun raising cattle and feed. This made for safe travel for white men across the entire Arizona territory. All of these bands, however, continued to raid their eternal enemies, the Mexicans, in spite of the United States' laws against this practice.

When Geronimo and his family returned to their home base in the mountains near Pinos Altos, he discovered that serious trouble had started with the miners. Mangas Coloradas was still honoring the agreement he made in Santa Fe not to wage war on the Americans. Geronimo, Victorio and Loco (headmen of the Warm Springs band) all urged Mangas to become more aggressive. The older leader refused— until he was trapped by miners and whipped. The following year, 1860, the bands united and agreed to wage war on the white miners and settlers.

❖ Civil War Starts ❖

The Apaches noticed a strange thing occurring. The United States Army was removing their troops from the forts they had built in Arizona. By 1861, the troops had orders to destroy their Arizona forts and march into eastern New Mexico. The American Civil War between the Union and the Confederacy had begun.[11]

Geronimo and other warrior leaders may have thought this was a chance to rid their homeland of both white miners and Mexican ranchers. Geronimo assisted in attacks on these settlements, as well as on an immigrant train making its way to California. They killed sixteen settlers and took their cattle and sheep, allowing only the women and children to escape.[12] From then on, Geronimo trusted no one but his own people.

Geronimo Fights America

During the decade of the 1860s, Apache leaders, including Geronimo, were forced to live with the growing expansion of white settlements in New Mexico and Arizona. Along with the white miners came ranchers and other businesspeople who were determined to dominate the Southwest. In Geronimo's autobiography, he gives a sketchy narrative of this decade. But we know that he was by nature not one to stand back and let the other Apache warriors fight alone. Geronimo was closely connected to Juh, Mangas, and Cochise, both as family and by experience in war. When these headmen got into trouble, we can assume Geronimo fought by their side.

Scholar David Roberts says:

> *We know that Geronimo may have helped torture to death the hostages Cochise hoped to trade for his relatives in 1861; we know with reasonable certainty that Geronimo fought in the crucial battle of Apache Pass in 1862, that he was part of the council that begged Mangas not to go to his doom at Pinos Altos in 1863.*[1]

When these headmen led a raid or needed the help of Geronimo and his warriors, we can assume Geronimo tried to join them.

❖Attack at Apache Pass❖

Geronimo, Cochise, and Mangas Coloradas, together with their warriors gathered for an attack at Apache Pass, that crucial road through southern Arizona, in the summer of 1862. Their scouts had reported that a large force of Union soldiers was coming into Arizona from California. The warriors stationed themselves behind rocks up the sides of the pass. This effectively cut off those coming from the west. They also prevented any traveler from reaching the sole source of fresh spring water in the entire area.

Major James Carleton arrived with his California Column (the name given his force of soldiers). He was accompanied by Captain Thomas Roberts, of the California Infantry, and Captain John Cremony, a familiar figure in Apacheria after his escorting of the Boundary Commission. Carleton and Roberts headed for the pass leading their mounted soldiers and two covered wagons full of cannons (called howitzers). Cannons that powerful had never been seen in Apacheria before. The rifle attack of the Apaches could not stand up to such artillery. So this company made it through to the spring. They sent back a group to warn Cremony and the others.

This team of messengers was attacked by a war party led by Mangas Coloradas himself. Apaches say that Geronimo also fought in this battle. Several troopers were shot, several got through, and one young soldier, Private John Teal, was trapped on a wounded horse. Teal later told Cremony that he shot an important Apache. The "prominent Indian" John Teal shot was Mangas Coloradas. Cremony later said, "I regret to add, the rascal survived his wound to cause us more trouble."[2]

Geronimo, Cochise, and Victorio all wanted to continue the war against "the bluecoats," the United States Cavalry. But Mangas Coloradas faced the fact that in each battle, some Apache warriors were lost, and often women and children were sold into slavery. Bluecoats, miners, and ranchers kept on coming. The white-eyes were "as numerous as the stars." The Apache could not stop them. In January 1863, Mangas Coloradas decided once more to make peace. When he went in with an Apache peace party, soldiers shot him, then took his scalp. While the soldiers went out to kill Mangas's party awaiting him, an Army surgeon committed an act that would live in infamy throughout the history of the Apache tribe. He cut off Mangas Coloradas's great head, boiled the flesh from the skull, and sent it to a professor in the East to study.[3]

Geronimo never forgot the moment when he heard the terrible news. Mangas Coloradas had been his mentor and headman. To be murdered under a flag of truce was horrible. To have his head cut off went completely against Apache spiritual beliefs. This left Mangas Coloradas alone in the spirit world without the part of his body that determined who he was. But Geronimo had no time to mourn. He was in charge.

Without arms and low on supplies, Geronimo had to track down some food. His warriors killed some cattle drivers to get some steers, then slaughtered and packed the meat. The band was attacked again and again by Army troops. The winter was "the coldest I ever knew," Geronimo said.[4]

◈ Desperate Times ◈

The band endured desperate times. Still, they survived. But Geronimo knew they needed help. He heard that his friend Victorio, headman of the Warm Springs band, had held a council with government agents and had been given supplies. He said: "Game was scarce in our range then, and since I had been

Kaotenay, a son of Victorio of the Warm Springs Apaches, was photographed in 1884, probably during a stay on the San Carlos reservation.

chief [of his band] I had not asked for rations from the government, nor did I care to do so, but we did not wish to starve."[5]

Geronimo took his people to Warm Springs, where Victorio shared what he had. Geronimo remained grateful to him for the rest of his life. Throughout 1864–65, the bands mainly kept the peace. Then the American Civil War ended, and the westward expansion began again. The effort to keep all Native Americans on government-selected reservations became official policy. For the next twenty years, Geronimo fought his own personal war for freedom—for the Apache way of living that he cherished beyond life itself.

In the winter of 1869–70, Geronimo's close friend Juh brought his wife, Ishton, and their children to stay with the Mimbrenos and Chiricahuas. Ishton was pregnant, and Juh wanted her to stay north of the border. This way she would not have to deliver her baby in the wilds of the Mexican Sierra Madres. But Ishton's labor was so severe that it seemed none of the medicine people could save her. Geronimo, always a great believer in his spirit power, went out and prayed throughout Iston's labor. On the morning of the fifth day, his spirit power spoke within him. Apaches later recalled that Geronimo received the message: "The child will be born and your sister will live; and you will never be killed with weapons, but live to old age." This spirit message came true.

— ◈ —

In the winter of 1869–70, Geronimo is said to have received a message from his spirit power. It told him he would live to an old age, and never be killed with weapons. At the age of seventy, Geronimo had maintained his physical strength and power.

Geronimo hurried to his sister, and found that her baby son was born. They called him Daklugie which means "forced his way through."[6]

Geronimo remained devoted to this boy, who eventually received an American education and translated Geronimo's autobiography. Later the boy was called "Asa" Daklugie. Geronimo was never killed by enemy weapons, and certainly lived to old age. Yet many years of battle still awaited him.

GERONIMO FIGHTS AGAINST RESERVATIONS

By 1870, many Americans were moving west to settle in Arizona and New Mexico. Stage coach routes and the telegraph, or "talking wire," criss-crossed this territory. There was no rail-road, however, and only one stagecoach a day crossed the desert between El Paso and San Diego. The Southwest was still a remote fron-tier, but settlers were arriving constantly.

◈Agents are Hired◈

The United States government determined that the members of the southwestern tribes should be trained to be farmers. They must be kept on reservations where they would be supervised. They must not continue hunting and raiding. Many officials in Washington believed that allowances of meat, blankets, and seeds would encourage the Native Americans to settle on these reservations. In 1869, with the support of President Ulysses S. Grant, agents were hired to "protect the Indian from abuses, as well as curb his tendency toward hostility."[1] Secretary of the Board of Peace Commissioners, Vincent Colyer of New York, was given power to deal with the Apaches. Most of these agents had no personal experience with Native Americans.

◈New Approach◈

Now that the Civil War was over, many men were accustomed to combat. They joined the cavalry to fight in the West. The Army had tried for years to conquer the Apaches. They had reduced their numbers through battles and disease. But they had failed to take control. General Sherman assigned General George Crook to command the forces to subdue the Apaches. Crook had been fighting the Sioux on the northern plains. In June 1871, he arrived in Tucson, Arizona, and devised a new military approach.[2] Crook decided that to track down and capture men like

— ◈ —

General George Crook, one of the most successful campaigners against the Native Americans, could not capture Geronimo in battle. Crook stands beside his mule. He is pictured with two Apache scouts known as Alchise and Dutchy.

Geronimo, you had to ride the same kind of horses and try the same warfare. To do this, you hired Native Americans to scout for you. You lived the same rough life on the trail. To catch Geronimo, you had to be just as determined to kill your enemy as he was. By November 1871, Crook wrote [Rutherford B. Hayes]:

> *If this entire Indian question be left to me . . . I have not the slightest doubt of my ability to conquer a lasting peace with this Apache race in a comparatively short period of time.*[3]

As far as we know, Geronimo was raiding Mexico during 1870-71. He does not state exactly where he operated at that time. About then, Victorio, of the Warm Springs band, and Cochise, of the Chiricahuas, tried to make peace with the Army. Both headmen knew they were giving up much of their territories to restrict themselves to these reservations. But their bands needed peace. So they took in as many of their numbers as would follow. Geronimo, reportedly, continued his raiding in Mexico.

Victorio's promised reservation turned out to be distant from the actual Warm Springs, high in the mountains on the Tularosa River. Because of its extreme altitude and bad water, his band could not grow crops. The meat promised to them did not come. The winter was grim. Cochise, however, seemed satisfied with his deal with the government.

◈General Howard Arrives◈

In the spring of 1872, a new military man, Major General O. O. Howard, arrived in Arizona. Noted for his strong Christian beliefs, Howard had been sent by more peace-oriented officials in Washington. His mission was to soften General Crook's proposed campaign of rigid confinement or extermination of the Apache people. Howard's arrival stopped Crook just as he was about to form a major attack on those Apaches who were not already confined. Howard called a council at Apache Pass with Apache leaders, including Geronimo. Although Geronimo had vowed never to trust another white man, he too joined the others in trusting General Howard. A treaty, which Geronimo is said to have signed, was made to keep peace at Apache Pass. Geronimo later said: "If there is any pure, honest white man in the United States Army, that man is General Howard. All the Indians respect him."[4]

For a while the Apaches tried to live on reservations together. But Geronimo's people grew restless. They left Apache Pass and spent time on Victorio's New Mexico reservation. Others went to the reservation at San Carlos. Juh's Nednai band probably returned to their mountain hideouts in Sonora, Mexico. Geronimo did not like the hard life with Victorio up on the Tularosa. Being contained went against his nature. This probably caused him to rejoin the Nednais and continue to raid out of Mexico.

❖New Agent Assigned❖

A new agent for the San Carlos reservation was assigned. He was an Easterner, John Clum, barely twenty-three years of age. Clum, although inexperienced, brashly told the soldiers guarding the reservation at San Carlos that he did not need military commanders. Clum decided to institute the first self-rule among the Apache people. He helped train Apache police and let them work to keep order. Warriors would use their guns for hunting. Otherwise, guns were checked with their native policemen. No tizwin (corn whiskey) was to be brewed. Amazingly, the western bands that were congregated on the San Carlos agreed.[5]

Agent Clum was then assigned to manage the Apache Pass reservation. The complex business of cross-management between the agents and the military caused trouble. General George Crook was sent north to lead more campaigns against the Sioux. Through 1875 Clum ran both reservations. He kept their farming and building projects in full swing. For the most part, a unified life for the bands at San Carlos seemed possible.

Agent Tom Jeffords told Clum that Geronimo, Juh, and another leader called Nolgee "reported regularly at the agency for their rations." We don't know how regularly Geronimo visited the reservation. Clum said:

I sent for the chiefs, and we had big smoke and big talk on June 8 [1876]. Geronimo related how he and his people had joined in the Cochise-Howard treaty, and now that the young chiefs were going to San Carlos, the southern Chiricahuas desired to go there also. His families, he said, were twenty miles distant, down near the Mexican line.[6]

Why these hostiles, or renegades, as they were now called by the army, came in to meet Clum, we do not know. Clum told Geronimo, Juh, and the others that they must relocate to the San Carlos reservation. Geronimo nodded, but he already had a secret plan to break out.

❖Geronimo Disappears❖

Geronimo persuaded Clum to give him and Juh written passes for twenty days. This would get them past the soldiers so they could assemble all of their family members. Clum argued Geronimo down to a four-day pass. He thought he had beaten the wily warrior. Geronimo, with Juh and the others, used that pass to get past the soldiers on the southern border. With great speed and secrecy, they vanished into Mexico—in under four days.[7]

Clum had failed to keep Geronimo confined on his reservation. After that, he blamed Geronimo for every raid conducted in the Southwest. Geronimo and the Nednais did continue to raid south of the border. They took mostly horses and some cattle. They then slipped back up to New Mexico, where they sold them to ranchers. They used the money to buy ammunition and food. Geronimo built a hideout near the Warm Springs reservation. There, for several years, he operated successfully, until 1877.

Geronimo was still using the now-peaceful Warm Springs reservation, and some of Victorio's band did not like that. One said:

> We were on friendly terms with the towns around us, and we were causing no trouble there. But the Central Chiricahua and the Southern Chiricahua [Nednais] came around. They used to bring horses stolen from the south, and they got us into trouble. But our leader, Victorio, wouldn't do anything about it. He said, "These people are not bothering us."[8]

Although he had renounced the warrior way, Victorio would not turn in his relatives Juh and Geronimo.

◈Geronimo Captured◈

Clum, who was four hundred miles away on the San Carlos reservation, took a force of native police and made the trip to the Alamosa. He had orders from the Commissioner on Indian Affairs to "take police and arrest renegade Indians at Southern Apache Agency . . . and hold them in confinement for murder and robbery" at San Carlos. The primary "renegade" was Geronimo. Clum admitted he needed the military for this maneuver. He requested three companies of cavalry to meet him at Warm Springs on April 21. Clum

— ◈ —

Agent John Clum (center) was the only man to ever capture Geronimo. He did so in 1877, using his Apache police force and trickery. Clum is pictured here at San Carlos, the Arizona reservation that he managed. Two Apaches named Diablo and Eskiminzin pose beside him.

and his police, however, arrived first. Quickly he sent a messenger to Geronimo's camp for a council. Geronimo assumed this was Victorio's idea, so he arrived with his wives and children. Suddenly they were surrounded by Apache police.

Geronimo later stated:

> Soldiers met us, disarmed us, and took us both to headquarters, where we were tried by court-martial. They asked us only a few questions, and then Victorio was released, and I was sentenced to the guardhouse. Scouts conducted me, . . . and put me in chains.[9]

After he became a newspaper editor, Clum wrote a description of Geronimo at the moment:

> He stood erect as a mountain pine, while every outline of his symmetrical form indicated strength and endurance. His abundant ebony locks draped his ample shoulders, his stern features, his keen piercing eye, and his proud and graceful posture combined to create in him the model of an Apache war-chief . . . a name and character dreaded by all. His eyes blazed . . . and his form quivered with suppressed rage.[10]

Clum took Geronimo's rifle and kept it until his own death many years later.

Geronimo continued: "I was kept a prisoner for four months, during which time I was transferred to San Carlos. I think I had another trial, although I was not present."[11]

Why was Geronimo not hanged for murder? We do not know. But Clum could not get permission from the government to do it. Clum's son, Woodworth, said in his father's biography: "Geronimo should have been hanged not later than August 1877. His record for murder and robbery was common knowledge." Clum stated that "Geronimo's shackles should never have been removed except to let him walk to the gallows."[12] John Clum got into a battle with the military and was himself removed. The agent who once said: "I am determined that the Apaches would get a square deal," had failed.

❖Geronimo is Freed❖

The following agent, Henry Hart, freed Geronimo and forced his people to live on San Carlos. Geronimo, then in his late fifties, tried to live this captive farmer's life. However, he said later: "We were not satisfied."[13] By the end of 1880, Victorio had been killed in a battle in Mexico. With Victorio dead and with most of the bands subdued on the San Carlos reservation, white settlers decided they had beaten the Apaches. They had apparently forgotten about Geronimo.

GERONIMO SURVIVES ON THE RUN

After the death of Victorio, Geronimo and his band joined the remaining Chiricahuas and Warm Springs Apaches, as well as some western bands. During 1880, with their numbers so reduced, they tried to make a life together on the San Carlos reservation in southeastern Arizona. Just north of San Carlos, on the old Fort Apache reservation, a native religious revival was occurring. A White Mountain Apache man called Nochay del klinne became a self-styled prophet. He conducted religious meetings, claiming to contact the great deceased Apache leaders. He predicted their resurrection, and promised better times to living Apaches.

❖Religious Revival❖

The Apaches in the area began to hear about Nochay del klinne. Many got swept up in his ceremonies. Great numbers traveled to Cibecue Creek to join in the prophet's dances.[1] Did Geronimo and Juh, genuine practitioners of the Apache religion, fall under the power of Nochay del klinne? According to Asa Daklugie, son of Juh and the nephew of Geronimo, his father and uncle did attend the dances in 1881. They were also present at the final fatal ceremony.[2]

Geronimo stated that Nochay del klinne told him about a marvelous visit to the spirit land of the dead.[3] Geronimo, who had a few near-death experiences when wounded in battle, was skeptical about this man. But he could not prevent the terrible misunderstanding on the part of the United States Army. Troops with Apache scouts invaded a ceremony on Cibicu Creek during August 1881. Fearing that the prophet was encouraging the Apaches to rise up against the government, the army attacked. Along with Nochay del klinne, eighteen Apaches died. Eight government soldiers were killed in the fight. Geronimo and Juh were apparently not injured.

After this incident, the army called in more troops to the area. Such a buildup made the Apache leaders nervous.[4] This and other factors caused Geronimo, the Chiricahuas, Juh, and the Nednais to consider breaking out of San Carlos. As usual, the Apaches did not receive what they had been promised. They were forbidden to roam and hunt game or find mescal fruit to bake. The past winter, with its small allotment of blankets and cloth for clothing, had been grim. General Crook wrote to the United States District Attorney complaining that the goods intended for the Apaches were stolen before anyone ever received them.

❖Breakout!❖

In spite of Crook's efforts to improve life for the San Carlos Apaches, the Apache people were still kept as imprisoned beggars. Along with Juh, Geronimo broke out on September 30, 1881. About seventy-five warriors with wives and children slipped away during the confusion of "ration day."[5] Loco, headman of the remaining Warm Springs band, refused to go. Regarding that time, Asa Daklugie said:

> Many, like Loco, had given up, even though they were brave, fighting men. They had given up so that those of their tribe who still lived might survive. There was only one leader remaining who did not give up and that was Geronimo.[6]

During the next four years, the Apaches would wage their final war against both Mexico and the United States. When Geronimo and his fellow

Apaches waged war, they still tried to observe their rituals. They attacked out of necessity. They planned their raids and prepared their weapons. During the pre-battle night, they danced. They properly dressed their hair and painted their faces and bodies for war. But the Apache were never an army.

❖A Warrior's Life❖

Geronimo and his men fought, moved, regrouped, and fought again, always taking their women, children, and elderly. Since they could seldom keep a permanent camp, their families had to be active participants in battle. Little boys became warrior's assistants; girls helped dig trenches and reload weapons. Women often fought alongside men. There were some tragic instances where, in order for the tribe to attack or escape undetected, an infant who cried had to be smothered. The Apache people had no food sources, supplies, or ammunition other than what they could trap or steal.

One Apache boy, later called Charlie Smith, recalled the rigorous training that Geronimo gave the boys. He said:

> *Geronimo would line the boys up on the bank, have us build a fire and undress by it, and then make us plunge into the stream, breaking the ice as we went . . . time after time, we warmed ourselves by the fire and returned to the icy water. There were times when I just hated him . . . Nobody defied Geronimo.*[7]

The boys learned that they had to grow into warriors quickly, if they were to stay free.

Loco and his Warm Springs band, those who remained of Victorio's group, would not live much longer on the San Carlos reservation. Nana, the elderly headman, had never come in after the murder of Victorio. When Geronimo and Juh took their people to join him in the Mexican Sierra Madres, they had a council. Geronimo stated that with summer coming (1882), Loco's people should come out before they died of hunger, heat, and insects. Nana reminded Geronimo: "Each Apache decides for himself whether or not he fights. We are a free people. We do not force men to fight . . ." Although he deferred to Nana, Geronimo, always the war leader, said about Loco: "He could be forced to leave."[8]

The son of Geronimo's cousin, Jason Betzinez, lived with Loco at the time. He claimed that the Chiricahua warriors went up to San Carlos, killed two of the scouts, and told Loco he would be blamed for it if he didn't come out and fight![9] Helpless and without weapons, Loco marched his people to Mexico, moving through the high mountain passes where cavalry could not follow.

Geronimo, described by Betzinez as "pretty much the main leader, most intelligent and resourceful, the most vigorous, and farsighted" also became the most brutal when it came to raids.[10] His war had reached the stage of kill or be killed. He took no prisoners.

Survivors of one of his raids lived to tell of Geronimo's brutality on the George Stevens ranch. Jimmie Stevens, George's young son, told the tale, colored with his hatred of Geronimo.

The Stevens sheep ranch was run by Victoriano Mestas, a Mexican who had been captured and lived some of his youth with Apaches. He knew Geronimo, who had treated him well.[11] Later Mestas was traded back to whites and married in the Mexican culture. When Geronimo arrived with his band of raiders at the Stevens' ranch, he asked for food and said they would leave without trouble. Bylas, an Apache herder from another band, stood up to him: "You lie, Geronimo, you want to kill us. Always you are a liar."[12] Mestas remembered Geronimo's kindness to him as a boy, and let the Chiricahuas, including Naiche, Chato, and Chihuahua, into the camp area. Mrs. Mestas cooked them all tortillas. They slaughtered some sheep to eat, and Geronimo killed Stevens's own colt to roast for meat. When it was time to leave, the ten Mexican herders grew careless.

At Geronimo's signal, the Mexicans were bound, including Mrs. Mestas and her children. One small son escaped unnoticed and hid beneath Mrs. Bylas' skirts. Naiche and Chato protested. "Why do you want to kill these people when you promised to do them no harm?" Chato asked Geronimo. Geronimo said nothing. Chihuahua said: "These people are Mexicans, they are our enemies." Geronimo nodded.

The herders were shot, even Mestas, his wife, and children. Then one boy crawled from beneath Mrs. Bylas's skirts, and was spotted by Geronimo.

But one of the Chiricahua warriors—some say it was Naiche—had enough killing. Jimmie Stevens claimed the warrior said: "I will kill any man who harms the little boy." Geronimo, who had lost at least four, if not more of his own children to Mexican guns, let the Mestas boy live.

❖Another Massacre❖

Sometime late in 1882, the remaining Apache bands joined in one camp. The count was estimated at several hundred Apaches, with some Navajos, Mexicans, and whites who had grown up captive and stayed with the Apaches.[13] Geronimo and Juh were principal leaders. Geronimo made the same mistake he had made back in 1850; he decided to trust the town of Casas Grandes to keep the peace for trading purposes. He left the families relatively unguarded. The same kind of ambush happened again. With many of the warriors drunk after trading, Mexican troops attacked them.

Geronimo and Juh fought back, but when the massacre ended, the troopers had killed twenty Apaches and carried thirty-five into slavery. One of the captives was Geronimo's wife of thirty years, Cheehashkish. Their grown children survived the battle.[14]

Geronimo tried many times over the years to recover Cheehashkish. But he never saw her again. Sometime after this loss, Geronimo, then almost sixty, married a young Nednai woman named Ziyeh. She stood by him for the rest of her life. They had two surviving children. Geronimo's wife Shegha supposedly also had a child at this time, but this child did not grow up. Also about this period, Geronimo married Ihtedda. Some scholars say she was a daughter of the headman Nana. She was later nicknamed Katie and was a survivor of the massacre that killed Victorio.[15] Charlie Smith said Ihtedda was a Mescalero girl who somehow was brought to Geronimo's camp. As the leader, Geronimo chose her for his wife.[16]

❖Life on the Run❖

In 1883, life on the run got even harder for the Apache people. Juh took his followers up to his remote camp for safety, but Geronimo and his people continued dangerous raiding. Later in the year, they reunited. When they did, Geronimo received terrible news: Juh's camp had been attacked. Mexican troops surprised them, captured, and killed many. Juh's wife, Ishton, and Juh's young daughter were murdered. Asa Daklugie survived, as did Juh's older sons and his daughter Jacali, whose knee was shattered with bullets.[17]

Later, Geronimo led a select group of warriors back to Casas Grande. They took Mexican hostages in hopes of trading them for their captives, including Cheehashkish. Geronimo and his band made camp with these captives. Suddenly Geronimo had one of his many spiritual visions.

Jason Betzinez, then a warrior's assistant to Geronimo, recalled that in the midst of eating, Geronimo dropped his knife and said: "Men, our people whom we left at our base camp are now in the hands of U.S. troops! What shall we do?[18] Geronimo had developed a powerful ability to consult his psychic power and see events happening far way. Sometimes he saw events about to happen, such as troops secretly advancing on them. General George Crook had indeed returned, led by a force of White Mountain Apache scouts. Geronimo's people were surrounded.

❖Time to Surrender❖

Geronimo had no choice this time. In May of 1883, he was forced to consider surrendering to General Crook. Bringing the Mexican women captives with him, he returned to camp. There Geronimo found that some of the Chiricahua men had hidden in the rocks, waiting to see if they could fight their way out. General Crook bravely went out alone, pretending to be hunting game. He thought that the Chiricahua men would negotiate with him and not feel they had surrendered. Geronimo spoke to him.[19] Crook put it plainly to the Apaches, asking them if they wanted peace or war? The next morning, Geronimo, Naiche, Chatto, and a fourth leader ate breakfast with Crook. The leaders decided they had better make peace. Crook sent the Mexican women captives home.

Making the return trip through hostile Mexican territory to the Arizona reservation was not going to be easy. Each Apache leader took responsibility for getting back to San Carlos with his own group. Crook did not have enough troops to protect them all. Juh and his band were still roaming the mountains in Mexico. Then Geronimo received more hard news. His lifetime friend and fellow leader in war, Juh of the Nednais, had died. Asa Daklugie reported it had been a stroke or heart attack.

❖Another Breakout❖

Geronimo was the last to leave freedom. He did not show up at San Carlos until February 1884. Life again was harsh on this reservation. So Geronimo broke out once more in May 1885. He claimed he heard Crook order soldiers to imprison or execute him. Crook denied this. Geronimo never believed him. He, along with Chihuahua, Naiche, Nana, Mangas, Perico, Fun, about thirty-five other men, eight youths, and ten women, took off for Sonora. His wife, Ziyeh, gave birth to their son Fenton at about this time.

Once again, General Crook and his forces tracked Geronimo down. His assistant, Lieutenant Britton Davis, who had been tracking and fighting Apaches

— ✦ —

Geronimo escaped from the San Carlos reservation many times. He was finally tracked down by Apache scouts working for the United States Army. This group of five scouts includes a man who called himself Mickey Free (upper row, far right). He was the boy named Felix Ward whose 1861 kidnapping was wrongly blamed on Cochise. This caused Cochise and Geronimo to wage war on white settlers.

since 1882, was in charge of the "Indan scouts." Davis had learned quickly the unique character of Apaches. "The difficulties of subduing the Apache were so unique that they were not understood even by many of our superior officers in Washington," he wrote. Regarding General Philip Sheridan, then in command of the United States Army, Davis said: "His ignorance of these matters led him to give orders that were impossible to carry out."[20]

General Crook again rounded up Geronimo and the Chiricahuas. He was making no deals. He trusted none of them. In March 1886, he wrote that the Apaches were:

> . . . though tired of the constant hounding of the campaign, in superb physical condition, armed to the teeth, and with an abundance of ammunition . . . fierce as so many tigers—knowing what pitiless brutes they are themselves, they mistrust everyone else . . . never more than five to eight men came into our camp at any one time.[21]

❖Return to Captivity❖

At the surrender conference on March 25, 1886, south of San Bernardino Springs, Mexico, Geronimo made a passionate speech. Protesting threats against him as reason for the last breakout, Geronimo said:

> Trouble has come from the agents and the interpreters. The Earth-Mother is listening to me and I hope that all may be so arranged that from

now on, there shall be no trouble and we shall always have peace.[22]

Crook insisted on surrender and prison, but the Apaches wanted to return to the reservation. Crook got them to agree to two years of prison exile in the East. However, when he wired General Sheridan in Washington, who consulted President Cleveland, the terms were refused! Sheridan wired back: "The President cannot assent to the surrender of the hostiles on the terms of their imprisonment East for two years with the understanding of their return to the reservation."

President Cleveland wanted unconditional surrender, sparing only their lives. Crook knew these terms were disastrous. He wired Sheridan the new terms would "not only make it impossible for me to negotiate with them, but result in their scattering to the mountains." Crook, as usual, was correct. Geronimo, Naiche, a band of twenty men, thirteen women, and sixty youngsters all took off for the mountains.

Geronimo later stated that the wife of Mangas and others "told me the Americans were going to arrest me and hang me, and so I left. I would like to know who it was that gave the order to arrest me and hang me. I was living peaceably there with my family."[23] Miscommunication may have been the answer.

In April 1886, General Nelson Miles, a tough "Indian fighter," was sent to replace General Crook.

— ✦ —

Castillo de San Marcos (The Fort Saint Marcos), completed by Spanish forces in 1695, was used to defend Spain's interests in Saint Augustine, Florida. The Apaches thought that they had a deal with General Nelson Miles that would allow them to return to the San Carlos reservation if they spent two years in a prison in the East such as this one. The National Park Service manages Castillo de San Marcos today.

Miles got rid of Native American police, and put in place almost five thousand white troopers. This huge force combed the Mexican mountains looking for Geronimo's small band. They failed to find them. Mounted troopers could never cross the mountain passes that Geronimo knew so well. During this last desperate few months, the Apaches roamed Sonora, Arizona, and New Mexico, often with no food or water.

Geronimo said of that time:

> We were reckless of our lives, because we felt that every man's hand was against us. If we returned to the reservation, we would be put in prison and killed; if we stayed in Mexico they would continue to send soldiers to fight us; so we gave no quarter to anyone and asked no favors.[24]

General Miles found a man capable of tracking and negotiating with Geronimo: Lieutenant Charles Gatewood. Gatewood had served for years with Crook. He understood the Apache nature and even learned some of their language. Geronimo seemed to have known and respected him.[25] With a selected force of scouts and only six soldiers, Gatewood carefully tracked Geronimo into Mexico. Gatewood knew that Apaches would respect courage. He walked alone into a council ground selected by women go-betweens. Geronimo brought his warriors in.

A long period of negotiating took place. Finally, Geronimo asked Gatewood serious questions about General Miles's trustworthiness. Then he asked

Gatewood what he would do if he were an Apache. Gatewood said: "I would trust General Miles and take him at his word."[26]

Geronimo knew Ziyeh had been taken by army scouts and sent on to a Florida prison. Ihtedda, pregnant with their daughter, had been captured by the army. Geronimo had only his wife Shegha left with him.

❖Surrender at Fort Bowie❖

Geronimo surrendered to General Nelson Miles at Fort Bowie, in the southeastern corner of Arizona, on September 4, 1886. A nephew of Geronimo's, Joseph Kanseah, said of this moment: "I know that he was lied to by Miles. That man did not do what he promised. Geronimo was a really great fighting man." As Charlie Smith put it:

> *Geronimo knew it was hopeless. But that did not stop him. I admire him for that. He was a great leader of men . . . don't forget he was fighting against enormous odds, and that nobody ever captured him.*[27]

Geronimo Sees the Twentieth Century

The surrendered bands of Apaches, including Geronimo and his warriors, were packed onto trains at Holbrook, Arizona, for their journey east. The trains were over-crowded and conditions were poor. The Apaches were treated like cattle. Most Apaches had never seen a train, and must have been suspicious of them. Teenager Jason Betzinez at first found the train trip an adventure: "We were greatly surprised to see one farm after another . . . and many more people. We had no idea there were so many whites."[1]

◈Torturous Trip◈

As the trip wore on in the September heat, it became gruelling. The 383 Apaches were crowded into ten old coach cars. The windows were sealed shut. According to witnesses, the heat and stench were gruesome, buckets used for latrines were rarely emptied, and clean water for washing was never offered.[2] At each stop, white settlers gathered and taunted the Apaches. Asa Daklugie said: "Every time [the train] stopped, we expected to be taken off and killed."[3]

Raymond Loco, descendant of the Chiricahua headman, Loco, claimed that his band was deprived of all personal belongings, and was forced to board the trains, dirty and nearly naked. As they rode, the smoke from the train leaked into the sealed cars. This caused motion sickness. After days of vomiting with no toilets or clean water, the coaches were so vile that they had to be hosed out. Sickness from bad food was rampant.[4]

◈"Hostiles" Separated◈

Geronimo and those termed "hostile" warriors were removed from the others and kept at San Antonio, Texas. For forty days, Geronimo said, the army "held me to be tried by their laws."[5] The

— ❖ —

Geronimo was sent to Florida with the rest of his band. This photo shows the captives together, as they endured the torturous train trip. Scholar Angie Debo identified those in the front row (from left to right) as: Fun, Perico, Naiche, Geronimo, Chappo, and a boy named Garditha. Army guards with rifles watch over them.

authorities discussed the terms of the supposed treaty given these Apaches by General Miles. Finally, it was decided: the warriors, such as Geronimo, Fun, Perico, Naiche, and the others would go on to prison in Pensacola, Florida. But most of their wives and children would be kept in another Florida fort. The promise of a return after two years to their reservation would be ignored. In fact, Geronimo would be a prisoner for life.

There is no photograph in print showing Geronimo smiling. His expression seems to be, by nature, serious. But a photograph taken of him awaiting his fate in San Antonio (see page 12) shows the stress he must have felt. In September 1886, Geronimo was about sixty-three. He looks strangely poised between the Apache and the American worlds: he wears an American banded hat, jacket, and cowboy boots over an Apache shirt, leggings, and breechcloth. Perhaps he sensed that he would never live the Apache life again.

❖Prison for Others❖

The "good Indians" who had cooperated with the army back in Arizona were sent, with most of the wives and children, to Fort Pickens on Santa Rosa Island off Pensacola, Florida. These seventy-five men and three hundred twenty-five women and children had stayed on the Fort Apache reservation and many

— ❖ —

Castillo de San Marcos (shown here) once housed Apache prisoners. Barred windows and doors sealed the damp interior rooms. Tourists in 1886 came to catch a glimpse of the Apache prisoners. A rusted iron plaque at the fort commemorates the imprisonment of the Apaches, stating: "Geronimo's band of seventy-seven Chiracahua Apaches captured in the west were imprisoned in this fort for thirteen months." The plaque does not mention the fact that Geronimo was probably not one of the prisoners.

had acted as army scouts.[6] A Florida prison was their reward.

Before Geronimo and the other hostiles arrived in Florida, the two cities that had places to keep them—St. Augustine and Pensacola—fought over who would get these tourist attractions. Many families were already imprisoned in the Castillo de San Marcos, called Fort Marion in English, at St. Augustine. St. Augustinians and Pensacolians each wanted Geronimo to be imprisoned in their city. Pensacolians started a petition to get him placed at Fort Pickens, where they claimed to have more space and privacy. Also, the locals could advertise him to tourists: "The painted demons . . . would be a better card than a circus or sea serpent."[7]

The War Department decided to put Geronimo and the other warriors in Fort Pickens at Pensacola. The town's newspaper stated:

> The government has selected the most suitable place to incarcerate the greatest living American general and his principal officers . . . We welcome the nation's distinguished guests.[8]

❖Diseases Invade❖

The humid climate immediately affected the health of people used to dry, high altitudes. Malarial fever (a highly contagious disease) broke out at Fort Marion, which crowded 502 people into quarters built for 150 soldiers.[9] By the end of September 1886, 152 people at the fort had been treated for the fever. The prisoners also had little clothing to protect them from the rain and insects.

During the winter of 1887, the public swarmed to see these celebrities from the Southwest. This contact with the public exposed the Apaches to new diseases. Serious health problems were also caused by the only latrine being sunk close beside the only drinking well. Although the sanitation and the climate were no better than at Fort Marion, and the winter winds colder, most of the families were sent over to Pensacola. At Fort Pickens, Geronimo and the Apaches became the big show of Santa Rosa Island. On a record day, 459 tourists sailed over to look at them.[10]

At Fort Marion, Ihtedda, who had become pregnant before Geronimo was taken prisoner, gave birth to their daughter Lenna there. Also in jail were Ziyeh and their son Fenton, who had been separated from Geronimo for two years. Sadly, Geronimo and Shegha lost their young daughter at the St. Augustine Fort.

In April 1887, the wives and children of Geronimo and the other warriors finally joined them at Fort Pickens. Shegha's health soon deteriorated. By September 1887, she died and was buried in a military cemetery, with Geronimo handling her funeral. Ihtedda and Ziyeh and their children survived.

❖Sickness Continues❖

Malaria, tuberculosis, and fevers also sickened the Apaches at Fort Pickens. Food rations were scarce, until their star prisoner Geronimo protested loudly. He also knew that making money might help his family survive. So he began playing the role of tourist attraction. He started selling personal items to eager Floridians, and kept the cash.

The government finally moved the Apaches to Mount Vernon Barracks, twenty-five miles up the river, inland from Mobile, Alabama.[11] Although the Floridians were angry to lose their big attractions, Alabamians were delighted to have them. A reporter for the *Mobile Register* wrote: "The placing of the Indians at Mt. Vernon will add greatly to the attractiveness of the place as a Sunday School picnic resort."[12]

From May 1888 until October 1894, the Apaches struggled to survive their imprisonment in a place with a climate that many claimed was even worse for them than the Florida coast. Eugene Chihuahua, son of the Chiricahua headman, later said about Mount Vernon:

> *It had been built in the 1830s and had been abandoned. We had thought anything would be better than Fort Marion with its rain, mosquitos, and malaria, but we were to find out that it was good in comparison with Mt. Vernon . . . we didn't know what misery was till they dumped us in those swamps.*[13]

Ziyeh gave birth to a daughter, Eva, in 1889 under these harsh conditions.

❖ "Indian School" ❖

During their imprisonment, many Apache children were forcibly sent to the United States Indian Industrial School in Carlisle, Pennsylvania. In the fall of 1886, ninety-five children from the families then at Fort Marion, and five from Fort Pickens who were of school age were shipped north to this national boarding school. Many children were already infected with tuberculosis, which is extremely contagious. During 1887, fifteen Apache children died, and during 1888, the number rose to twenty-seven. Each year, more were lost from complications of tuberculosis, pneumonia, and malaria.[14]

Having never been separated from their children, the Apache adults worried constantly. One of the most famous students to be removed was Chappo Geronimo, son of Geronimo and his lost wife Cheehaskish. At age twenty-two, Chappo had seen his own wife and baby die in captivity. According to photos, Chappo was a strong and handsome man when he went to Carlisle in 1888. During his six years of study, he too got tuberculosis. When it was certain that he would not survive, Chappo was sent back to Mount Vernon barracks to die in Geronimo's arms. It is hard to know with certainty whether these young people would have taken ill if they had remained in prison with their parents, or whether life at the school was even worse for them. But die they did.

Geronimo saw a chance, however, to save his Mescalero wife Ihtedda. Those Apaches of Mescalero descent were allowed to return to New Mexico to a small reservation. It is said that Ihtedda, again pregnant, begged not to leave her husband. But Geronimo was firm. He had seen too many wives die. He insisted that Ihtedda and Lenna go home to safety and relative freedom. Ihtedda and Geronimo's son, Robert, was born in New Mexico. Robert and Lenna were not able to resume their relationship with their father for many years. But they did grow to adulthood.

❖Conditions Horrible❖

Geronimo continued to petition for a better prison situation. He said: "I longed in vain for the implements, house and stock that General Miles had promised me." No one in the Southwest, however, wanted these Apaches back within their borders. An interested party was also trying to relocate the Apaches: Lieutenant Guy Howard of the Twelfth Infantry, and an aide to his father, General O. O. Howard. Lieutenant Howard continued his father's sincere concern for the Apache people. He made a report which listed the medical conditions by the end of 1889 in Alabama, and said: "The three hundred and eighty-eight . . . at Mount Vernon Barracks are now in a condition which needs prompt action to avoid

— ❖ —

*The Apaches were kept in canvas tents at Mount Vernon
Barracks. Geronimo is shown standing in the center of the
photo. Scholar Henrietta Stockel states that these tents were
later burned to destroy the contagion from tuberculosis and
other diseases killing the Apaches.*

positive inhumanity."[15] Lieutenant Howard stated that the army medical officers believed the primary cause of Apache death was the "moist atmosphere of the sea coast." But no one seemed to know where to relocate them.

The Comanches and Kiowas then agreed to turn over a section of their reservation land in Oklahoma to be used by these long-exiled bands. The army outpost on this reservation was called Fort Sill. The army officers there would be in charge of Geronimo's band. Although the whites in the area were not pleased, no one looked for another solution. The Oklahoma reserve was higher and dryer. Perhaps the few living Chiricahuas could be saved.

❖To Oklahoma❖

Geronimo left his dead family members buried in Florida and Alabama, and took Ziyeh, Fenton, and Eva to a better prison life in Oklahoma. On October 4, 1894, the remnants of the Apaches arrived—only two hundred ninety-six people (forty-five students were at boarding school)—with no livestock and hardly a single possession. Hundreds of Kiowas and Comanches came to greet them. They could not speak the same language, however. So boys who had been to boarding school communicated in English.[16]

Along with Geronimo's wife and children, other relatives settled with him at Fort Sill. His brother Perico, sister Nahdoste, cousin Nahthletla and her son Jason Betzinez, as well as aging leaders Chihuahua, Nana, and Loco were all there. They all had to work and learn farming. They were still prisoners, but had private quarters and could resume Apache ceremonial life.

Geronimo, now past seventy, remained hardy in body and mind. He helped raise Fenton and Eva, as well as Dohnsay's boy, Tom, and girl, Nina, and worked the melon fields. As a prisoner of the United States government, he had to farm and depend on government issue. It would appear, however, that his growing status as a celebrity became apparent to him. He was constantly asked to do personal appearances. The officials at Fort Sill let him go to appear in exhibitions, such as the Omaha Trans-Mississippi Exposition of 1898.

The Omaha promoters had Geronimo sell his autographed photos, bows, and arrows. Then they surprised him with a meeting with General Nelson Miles, the officer whom he trusted at his surrender. Recalling the broken promises, Geronimo said: "You said that I would be forgiven. You lied to us, General Miles." Miles replied: "I did lie to you . . . but I learned to lie from you, Geronimo . . ." Geronimo stated that he had been kept from his Arizona homeland for twelve years, and the land wished him to return. Miles laughed and said the people of Arizona did not want him to return. Geronimo never saw Miles again.[17]

◈ Raising Money ◈

Although a prisoner, somehow Geronimo got his own bank account. All produce and stock raised by the Apaches on Fort Sill had to be sold by the government, with profits going into a general fund. But Geronimo's personal earnings were kept to himself. During the last years of his life, he accumulated over $10,000, a sizeable fortune at the turn of the century.[18]

Apaches, like people the world over, enjoyed games, competitions, races, and exciting forms of gambling. Males once played the game of "hoop and pole" and raced horses. At Fort Sill, the men still found time for games. Geronimo, always a fierce gambler, learned card games like poker and monte. He played expertly and loved to win! He could no longer race as a jockey due to his age and weight. Often he asked his wife, Ziyeh, (who was younger and lighter) to ride for him. Many Apaches of those times recalled Ziyeh, her hair bound tightly, racing Geronimo's horse.[19] Geronimo would also compete in shooting contests, and often won.

◈ Growing Fame ◈

With his growing fame, Geronimo was painted by artist Elbridge Burbank, financed by the Field Museum of Chicago. He was interviewed by historian Norman S. Wood for his book, *Lives of Famous Indian Chiefs*, in 1905. He became friends with Quannah Parker, famous headman of the Comanches, who often spent time in nearby Cache. Also in 1905, Geronimo began dictating his autobiography to S. M. Barrett, Superintendent of Education of the nearby town of Lawton. The book was translated by Asa Daklugie. This book would be the first-hand account of the Apache wars from the Native American viewpoint.

Tuberculosis claimed another victim close to Geronimo. In 1904 his wife Ziyeh died. By the end of 1905, Geronimo married an Apache widow, Souche, called Mary Loto in English. The marriage did not work out. By the summer of 1906, Souche was gone. Geronimo said: "She went home to her people—that is an Apache divorce."[20] Geronimo married again. His wife's name was Azul, and she lived to mourn Geronimo at his death.

❖ "Womanhood Dance" ❖

During these years, Geronimo's daughter Eva passed puberty. He was able to give her the most important ceremony for every Apache female, her "womanhood dance." Girls were given beautiful beaded dresses and were honored with songs and dances and feasting to celebrate their coming of age.

❖ World's Fair ❖

Geronimo joined many other Native Americans to appear and perform at the 1904 Louisiana Purchase

Exposition, often called the World's Fair, in St. Louis. Worried about being put together with other Native Americans who were traditionally the enemies of Apaches, Geronimo asked for "good attention and protection."[21] He got it. During his six months in residence in St. Louis, Geronimo lived in an "Indian village." There, many Native Americans demonstrated and sold their crafts. He made bows and arrows, then autographed them as well as photographs. The great war leader had passed from enemy to prisoner to exhibitor in the eyes of the white world.

Geronimo recorded his observations in his autobiography. He claimed that many St. Louis citizens invited him to come to their homes—"but my keeper always refused." On Sundays, Geronimo rode and roped in a "Wild West show." He saw men from around the world do amazing magic tricks. He observed moving pictures, glass blowers, machines, wonders of the new century.

At the Fair, Geronimo enjoyed a special experience. He became close to another participant, his daughter Lenna from New Mexico. His son Robert also visited him. Geronimo concluded at the Fair that he learned much about the white race: "They are a very kind and peaceful people. During all the time I was at the Fair, no one tried to harm me in any way."[22]

Geronimo was still physically powerful enough to make one more attempt to get imprisoned Apaches moved back to Arizona. Along with Quannah Parker and some chiefs from the Blackfoot, Ute, and Sioux tribes, Geronimo journeyed to Washington to ride in the 1905 inaugural parade of Theodore Roosevelt. All reports indicate that the crowds cheered Geronimo as loudly as they did the new president. Ironically, one member of the parade committee was Woodworth Clum, son of agent John Clum, the only man who ever got Geronimo in chains, and lived to see him released to raid again. Clum asked Roosevelt why he would include Geronimo, "the greatest single-handed murderer in American history?" Roosevelt supposedly said: "I wanted to give the people a good show."[23]

Geronimo had other motives besides earning money and selling his autographed mementos. He wanted to ask President Roosevelt to allow the Apaches to return to Arizona. He asked, and ended by saying:

> My heart is no longer bad. I will tell my people to obey no chief but the Great White Chief. I pray you to cut the ropes and make me free. Let me die in my own country, an old man who has been punished enough and is free.[24]

Roosevelt said he was sorry, but hatred still existed in Arizona against Geronimo. His return would cause bloodshed.

◈Geronimo Dies◈

Geronimo died a prisoner. One cold winter day in February 1909, he rode his horse to Lawton, Oklahoma, to sell some bows and arrows that he had made. There, he persuaded a soldier to buy him some whiskey. Riding home alone after dark in the severe cold, Geronimo took a fall from his horse and lay freezing for the rest of the night. He was found by his neighboring Apaches and taken home. His relatives refused to put him in the hospital, a place they feared. He died of pneumonia on February 15, 1909. Asa Daklugie held his hand as he died and said his last words were that he regretted his surrender. He said he should have stayed in Mexico and fought until the last man died.[25]

Geronimo lived at least eighty-five years. He had begun life as a hunter, healer, and a spiritual man. He saw the world of the Apache warrior change with the invasion of the Mexican slavers and scalp hunters. He saw the peaceful mountains and rugged deserts, promised to him by his god, blasted by miners and divided up by white cattle ranchers. He saw his wives, relatives, and children murdered during battles, stolen into slavery, or killed by white diseases. He survived over forty years of active war against those he considered his mortal enemies. He was captured only once, by trickery. He was never taken in battle. Once a prisoner, he quickly learned the white customs and currency—and survived twenty-three years of incarceration and hard labor to die fairly rich and extremely famous.

All Geronimo wanted, according to his own words, was to live free and die in the Apache homeland. He was willing to accept new laws, occupy much less land, as long as it was home:

> We could have plenty of good cultivating land, plenty of grass, plenty of timber, and plenty of minerals in that land which the Almighty created for the Apaches. It is my land, my home, my father's land.... I want to spend my last days there and be buried among those mountains . . . I might die in peace, feeling that my people . . . would increase in numbers, rather than diminish as at present, and that our name would not become extinct.[26]

❖A Lasting Legacy❖

Geronimo's name has become the symbol of the warrior who would not give up. "Geronimo!" was the battle cry of American soldiers throughout every war in the twentieth century. His people are thriving. Most live in Oklahoma or on reservations in New Mexico. They are proud of their tie to their Apache leader, Goyahkla, known as Geronimo. A modern Apache, world-famous sculptor Alan Houser, said in 1991 of Geronimo and the Chiricahua fight for freedom: "Geronimo called my dad cousin and my dad knew Geronimo's medicine songs . . . I often wonder about the fact that we were the only ones of the . . . group who stood up and said this is my land. We were the only ones who were brave enough to say that's enough."[27] Houser and the Apaches did not forget Geronimo. Although he did not live to see it, Geronimo's life-long war for Apache freedom was never fought in vain.

❧ CHRONOLOGY ❧

1823 ❖ Estimated date Geronimo (Apache name Goyahkla) is born to Juana and Taklishim.

1843 ❖ Estimated date Geronimo marries first wife Alope; their three children are born between 1843–1850.

1848 ❖ The Treaty of Guadalupe Hidalgo is ratified, transferring ownership of Apache homelands to the United States government.

1850 ❖ Geronimo, Juana, Alope and the children travel to trade at Janos, Chihuahua, Mexico. All but Geronimo are murdered by Sonoran militia.

1850 ❖ Geronimo unites Apache bands in battle against Sonoran militia; victorious, he is named "Geronimo."

1851 ❖ Geronimo marries second wife Cheehashkish; they have two children, Chappo and Dohnsay.

1851 ❖ Geronimo marries third wife Nanathathtith; they have one child.

1852 ❖ Geronimo's third wife and her child are killed by invasion of Mexican troops.

1860 ❖ Estimated date Geronimo marries fourth wife Shegha, relative of Chiricahua headman Cochise. Geronimo begins battling United States Army troops.

1863 ❖ Mangas Coloradas, headman of Geronimo's band, is captured and beheaded; Geronimo takes charge of band.

1874 ❖ After Cochise's death, western Apache bands are put on San Carlos Reservation.

1876 ✦ Geronimo and Juh bring their bands to San Carlos. Geronimo soon breaks out.

1880 –81 ✦ Geronimo tries to live on San Carlos reservation.

1881 –82 ✦ Geronimo escapes to the Sierra Madres hideout of Juh.

1882 ✦ Wife Cheehashkish is taken in battle with Mexican troops and sold into slavery.

1883 ✦ Geronimo married fifth wife Ziyeh of the Nednais; wife Shegha has a child.

1884 –85 ✦ Geronimo surrenders to General George Crook after being surrounded in Mexico. He returns to San Carlos Reservation. Wife Ziyeh has son Fenton and daughter Eva.

1885 ✦ Geronimo marries sixth wife Ihtedda, a Mescalero captive.

1885 –86 ✦ Geronimo again breaks out and lives in Mexico.

1886 ✦ Geronimo surrenders to General Nelson Miles on the promise of prison for two years, then reservation life.

1887 ✦ Shegha and child die of disease in Florida.

1888 –94 ✦ Geronimo and families survive at Mount Vernon Barracks, Mobile, Alabama. Ihtedda is sent back to New Mexico.

1894 ✦ Geronimo and all remaining Apaches sent as prisoners to Fort Sill, Oklahoma.

1904 ✦ After death of Ziyeh, Geronimo marries seventh wife Sousche (who leaves him) and eighth wife Azul, who survives him. Geronimo appears at St. Louis Worlds Fair.

1909 ✦ On February 15, Geronimo dies of pneumonia in Fort Sill.

CHAPTER NOTES

Chapter 1

1. Russell Shorto, *Geronimo and the Struggle for Apache Freedom* (Englewood Cliffs, N.J.: Silver Burdett Press, 1989), p. 12.

2. Jason Betzinez, *I Fought with Geronimo* (Lincoln, Nebr.: University of Nebraska Press, 1987), pp. 14–15.

3. Angie Debo, *Geronimo: The Man, His Time, His Place* (Norman, Okla.: University of Oklahoma Press, 1989), p. 34.

4. Donald E. Worchester, *The Apaches* (Norman, Okla.: University of Oklahoma Press, 1979; 1992 edition), pp. 9–10.

5. Dan L. Thrapp, *The Conquest of Apacheria* (Norman, Okla.: University of Oklahoma Press, 1967), pp. 8–9.

6. Geronimo, *Geronimo's Story of His Life*, edited by S. M. Barrett (New York: Duffield & Company, 1915), pp. 37–38.

7. Alexander B. Adams, *Geronimo: A Biography* (New York: G. P. Putnam's Sons, 1971), pp. 80–81.

8. Barrett, p. 44.

9. Ibid.

10. David Roberts, *Once They Moved Like the Wind: Cochise, Geronimo, and the Apache Wars* (New York: Simon & Schuster Touchstone, 1993) pp. 109–110.

11. Barrett, p. 45.

12. Debo, p.8.

13. Worcester, p. xvi.

14. Barrett, p. 46.

15. Ibid. p. 45.

16. Ibid. p. 25.

17. Debo, p. 38.

18. Barrett, p. 52.

19. Ibid. pp. 53–54.

20. Ibid. p. 55.

Chapter 2

1. Angie Debo, *Geronimo: The Man, His Time, His Place* (Norman, Okla.: University of Oklahoma Press, 1989), p. 8.

2. Jason Betzinez, *I Fought with Geronimo* (Lincoln, Nebr.: University of Nebraska Press, 1987), p. 14.

3. David Roberts, *Once They Moved Like the Wind: Cochise, Geronimo, and the Apache Wars* (New York: Simon & Schuster Touchstone, 1993), p. 104.

4. Eva Ball, *In the Days of Victorio* (Tucson, Ariz.: University of Arizona Press, 1990), p. 17.

5. Morris Edward Opler, *An Apache Life-Way* (Chicago: University of Chicago Press, 1941), pp. 10–11.

6. Ibid. p. 12.

7. Ibid. pp. 15–17.

8. Ball, p. 17.

9. Alexander Adams, *Geronimo* (New York: G. P. Putnam's Sons, 1971), p. 47.

10. Opler, p. 67.

11. Donald E. Worcester, *The Apaches* (Norman, Okla.: University of Oklahoma Press, 1992), p. xv.

12. Frank C. Lockwood, *The Apache Indians* (New York: Macmillan Company, 1938), p. 58.

13. Geronimo, *Geronimo's Story of His Life*, edited by S. M. Barrett (New York: Duffield & Company, 1915), p. 31.

14. Ball, p. 28.

15. Worcester, pp. 37–38.

16. Lockwood, p. 60.

17. Betzinez, p. 15.

18. Ibid.

19. Ibid.

20. Barrett, p. 36.

21. Worcester, pp. 42–43.

Chapter 3

1. Edgar Wyatt, *Geronimo: Last Apache War Chief*, Illustrated by Allan Houser (New York: McGraw-Hill Book Company, Inc., 1952), pp. 53–59.

2. Morris Edward Opler, *An Apache Life-Way* (Chicago: University of Chicago Press, 1941), p. 164.

3. Ibid., p. 162.

4. Donald E. Worchester, *The Apaches* (Norman, Okla.: University of Oklahoma Press, 1992) p. 43.

5. Ibid., p. 74.

6. Frank C. Lockwood, *The Apache Indians* (New York: Macmillan Company, 1938), p. 77.

7. Worchester, p. 44.

8. Angie Debo, *Geronimo: The Man, His Time, His Place* (Norman, Okla.: University of Oklahoma Press, 1989), p. 33.

9. Geronimo, *Geronimo's Story of His Life*, edited by S. M. Barrett (New York: Duffield & Company, 1915), pp. 113–114.

10. John C. Cremony, *Life Among the Apaches* (Tucson, Ariz.: Arizona Silhouettes, 1915 reprint of 1868 edition), p. 33.

11. Ibid.

12. Ibid., p. 34.

13. John Russell Bartlett, *Personal Narrative of Explorations and Incidents in Texas, New Mexico, California, Sonora and Chihuahua, Connected with the United States and Mexican Boundary Commission*, Vol. 1 (Chicago: Rio Grande Press, Inc., 1965 reprint of the 1854 edition), pp. 319–320.

14. Barrett, pp. 3–11.

Chapter 4

1. David Roberts, *Once They Moved Like the Wind: Cochise, Geronimo and the Apache Wars* (New York: Simon & Schuster Touchstone, 1993), p. 117.

2. Angie Debo, *Geronimo: The Man, His Time, His Place* (Norman, Okla.: University of Oklahoma Press, 1989), p. 47.

3. Eve Ball, *Indeh: An Apache Odyssey* (Norman, Okla.: University of Oklahoma Press, 1988), p. 61.

4. Dan L. Thrapp, *The Conquest of Apacheria* (Norman, Okla: University of Oklahoma Press, 1967), p. 13.

5. Ball, p. 90.

6. Geronimo, *Geronimo's Story of His Life*, edited by S. M. Barrett (New York: Duffield & Company, 1915), pp. 69–76.

7. Debo, p. 63.

8. Russell Shorto, *Geronimo and the Struggle for Apache Freedom* (Englewood Cliffs, N.J.: Silver Burdett Press, 1989), p. 42.

9. Donald E. Worcester, *The Apaches* (Norman, Okla.: University of Oklahoma Press, 1992), p. 73.

10. Worcester, p. 80.

11. Debo, pp. 61–62.

Chapter 5

1. David Roberts, *Once They Moved Like the Wind: Cochise, Geronimo, and the Apache Wars* (New York: Simon & Schuster Touchstone, 1993), p. 120.

2. Ibid.

3. Dan L. Thrapp, *The Conquest of Apacheria* (Norman, Okla.: University of Oklahoma Press, 1967), p. 22.

4. Geronimo, *Geronimo's Story of His Life*, edited by S. M. Barrett (New York: Duffield & Company, 1915), pp. 121–125.

5. Ibid.

6. Ibid.

Chapter 6

1. Dan L. Thrapp, *The Conquest of Apacheria* (Norman, Okla.: University of Oklahoma Press, 1967), p. 102.

2. Ibid., p. 95.

3. Ibid., p. 106.

4. Eve Ball, *In the Days of Victorio* (Tucson, Ariz.: University of Arizona Press, 1990 edition), pp. 48–49.

5. Donald E. Worcester, *The Apaches* (Norman, Okla.: University of Oklahoma Press, 1992), pp. 177–180.

6. Woodworth Clum, *Apache Agent*, (Lincoln, Nebr.: University of Nebraska Press, 1978), p. 180.

7. Alexander B. Adams, *Geronimo: A Biography* (New York: G. P. Putnam's Sons, 1971), pp. 199–200.

8. Morris Edward Opler, *An Apache Life-Way* (Chicago: University of Chicago Press, 1941), p. 462.

9. Geronimo, *Geronimo's Story of His Life*, edited by S. M. Barrett (New York: Duffield & Company, 1915), p. 131.

10. Russell Shorto, *Geronimo and the Struggle for Apache Freedom* (Englewood Cliffs, N.J.: Silver Burdett Press, 1989) p. 93.

11. Angie Debo, *Geronimo: The Man, His Time, His Place* (Norman, Okla.: University of Oklahoma Press, 1989), p. 114.

12. Clum, p. 263.

13. Barrett, p. 133.

Chapter 7

1. Dan L. Thrapp, *The Conquest of Apacheria* (Norman, Okla.: University of Oklahoma Press, 1967), pp. 217–218.

2. Angie Debo, *Geronimo: The Man, His Time, His Place* (Norman, Okla.: University of Oklahoma Press, 1989), p. 128.

3. Geronimo, *Geronimo's Story of His Life*, edited by S. M. Barrett (New York: Duffield & Company, 1915), pp. 208–211.

4. Dan L. Thrapp, *General Crook and the Sierra Madre Adventure* (Norman, Okla.: University of Oklahoma Press, 1972), pp. 26–27.

5. Alexander B. Adams, *Geronimo: A Biography* (New York: G. P. Putnam's Sons, 1971), p. 219.

6. Eve Ball, *Indeh: An Apache Odyssey* (Norman, Okla.: University of Oklahoma Press, 1988), p. 77.

7. Ibid., p. 103.

8. Eve Ball, *In the Days of Victorio* (Tucson, Ariz.: University of Arizona Press, 1990 edition), pp. 137–138.

9. Jason Betzinez, *I Fought with Geronimo* (Lincoln, Nebr.: University of Nebraska Press, 1987), pp. 56–67.

10. Ibid., p. 58.

11. Debo, p. 140.

12. Rose Santee, *Apache Land* (New York: Charles Scribner's Sons, 1947), pp. 167–168.

13. Betzinez, pp. 76–77.

14. Debo, pp. 156–157.

15. James L. Haley, *Apaches: A History and Culture Portrait* (New York: Doubleday & Company, 1981), p. 331.

16. Ball, *Indeh*, p. 103.

17. Ball, *Victorio*, pp. 146–147.

18. Betzinez, p. 113.

19. Thrapp, *General Crook*, pp. 157–158.

20. Britton Davis, *The Truth About Geronimo* (New Haven: Yale University Press, 1929), p. 74.

21. Thrapp, *Conquest*, pp. 343–344.

22. Davis, pp. 200–201.

23. Davis, p. 201.

24. Barrett, p. 141.

25. David Roberts, *Once They Moved Like the Wind: Cochise, Geronimo, and the Apache Wars* (New York: Simon & Schuster Touchstone, 1993), p. 290.

26. Ibid., p. 294.

27. Ball, *Indeh*, pp. 104–105.

Chapter 8

1. Jason Betzinez, *I Fought With Geronimo* (Lincoln, Nebr.: University of Nebraska Press, 1987), p. 142.

2. H. Henrietta Stockel, *Survival of the Spirit: Chiricahua Apaches in Captivity* (Reno, Nev.: University of Nevada Press, 1993), p. 78.

3. Sharon S. Magee, "The Selling of Geronimo," *Arizona Highways*, August 1995, Vol. 71, No. 8, p. 14.

4. Stockel, pp. 79–80.

5. Geronimo, *Geronimo's Story of His Life*, edited by S. M. Barrett (New York: Duffield & Company, 1915), p. 177.

6. Britton Davis, *The Truth About Geronimo* (New Haven: Yale University Press, 1929), p. 233.

7. Magee, p. 15.

8. Ibid.

9. Stockel, p. 86.

10. Magee, p. 15.

11. Ibid., p. 18.

12. Ibid.

13. Eve Ball, *Indeh: An Apache Odyssey* (Norman, Okla.: University of Oklahoma Press, 1988), pp. 138–139.

14. Stockel, p. 125.

15. Ibid., p. 160.

16. Angie Debo, *Geronimo: The Man, His Time, His Place* (Norman, Okla.: University of Oklahoma Press, 1989), pp. 364–365.

17. Roberts, p. 307.

18. Geronimo, *Geronimo's Story of His Life*, edited by S. M. Barrett (New York: Duffield & Company, 1915), p. 80–81.

19. Debo, p. 383.

20. Ibid., p. 391–392.

21. Barrett, p. 197.

22. Ibid., p. 205.

23. Woodworth Clum, *Apache Agent* (Lincoln, Nebr.: University of Nebraska Press, 1978), pp. 291–292.

24. Roberts, pp. 311–312.

25. Ibid., p. 314.

26. Barrett, p. 215.

27. Stockel, p. 251.

GLOSSARY

◈**botanist**—A scientist who studies plants and plant life.

◈**breechcloth**—A simple cloth that passes between the legs and falls in back and in front from a belt around the waist.

◈**cradleboard**—An infant carrier.

◈**howitzer**—A short cannon that shoots shells at a high angle of fire.

◈**malaria**—A disease carried by mosquitoes, caused by bacteria.

◈**mineralogist**—A scientist who studies minerals.

◈**New Mexico Territory**—The term for what is now all of New Mexico and Arizona.

◈**Old Mexico**—The term for the states of Chihuahua and Sonora in Mexico.

◈**pneumonia**—An inflammation of the lungs.

◆**shaman**—A specially trained medicine person who performed all Apache religious rites.

◆**tipi**—A wood frame covered with animal hides to form a sturdy tent.

◆**tuberculosis**—A highly contagious disease of the lungs.

◆**tumpline**—A strong strap to which the cradleboard could be attached.

◆**wickiup**—A simple shelter of saplings and brush that the Apaches built when they moved to follow the herds of game during warm weather.

☥⟿BIBLIOGRAPHY⟿☥

Adams, Alexander. *Geronimo*. New York: G. P. Putnam's Sons, 1972.

Ball, Eve. *In the Days of Victorio*. Tucson, Ariz.: University of Arizona Press, 1990 edition.

———. *Indeh, An Apache Odyssey*. Norman, Okla.: University of Oklahoma Press, 1988.

Bartlett, John Russell. *Personal Narrative of Explorations and Incidents in Texas, New Mexico, California, Sonora and Chihuahua, Connected with the United States and Mexican Boundary Commission*. Vol. 1. Chicago: Rio Grande Press, Inc., 1965 edition.

Betzinez, Jason. *I Fought With Geronimo*. Lincoln, Nebr.: University of Nebraska Press, 1987 edition.

Clum, Woodworth. *Apache Agent*. Lincoln, Nebr.: University of Nebraska Press, 1978.

Cremony, John C. *Life Among the Apaches*. Tucson, Ariz.: Arizona Silhouettes, 1915 reprint.

Davis, Britton. *The Truth about Geronimo*. Lincoln, Nebr.: University of Nebraska, 1976 reprint of 1929 edition.

Debo, Angie. *Geronimo: The Man, His Time, His Place*. Norman, Okla.: University of Oklahoma Press, 1989 edition.

Faulk, Odie B. *The Geronimo Campaign*. New York: Oxford University Press, 1969.

Geronimo. *Geronimo's Story of His Life*. edited by S. M. Barrett. New York: Duffield and Company, 1915.

Haley, James L. *Apaches: A History and Culture Portrait*. New York: Doubleday and Company, 1981.

Howard, Major General Oliver Otis. *My Life and Experiences Among Our Hostile Indians*. Hartford, Conn.: A. D. Worthington & Company, 1907.

Lockwood, Frank C. *The Apache Indians*. New York: Macmillan Company, 1938.

Magee, Sharon S. "The Selling of Geronimo." *Arizona Highways*, Vol. 71, No. 8, August 1995.

Opler, Morris Edward. *An Apache Life-Way*. Chicago: University of Chicago Press, 1941.

Roberts, David. *Once They Moved Like the Wind: Cochise, Geronimo, and the Apache Wars*. New York: Simon & Schuster Touchstone, 1993.

Santee, Rose. *Apache Land.* New York: Charles Scribner's Sons, 1947.

Shorto, Russell. *Geronimo and the Struggle for Apache Freedom.* Englewood Cliffs, N.J.: Silver Burdett Press, 1989.

Stockel, H. Henrietta. *Survival of the Spirit: Chiricahua Apaches in Captivity.* Reno, Nev.: University of Nevada Press, 1993.

Thrapp, Dan L. *The Conquest of Apacheria.* Norman, Okla.: University of Oklahoma Press, 1967.

————. *General Crook and the Sierra Madre Adventure.* Norman, Okla.: University of Oklahoma Press, 1972.

————. *Victorio and the Mimbrenos Apaches.* Norman, Okla.: University of Oklahoma Press, 1974.

Worcester, Donald E. *The Apaches.* Norman, Okla.: University of Oklahoma Press, 1992.

Wyatt, Edgar. *Geronimo: Last Apache War Chief.* Illustrated by Allan Houser. New York: McGraw-Hill Book Company, 1952.

⇒ INDEX ⇐